voice and the young actor: a workbook and dvd

RENA COOK

ILLUSTRATED BY
CAREY HISSEY

DVD DESIGNED AND CREATED BY
ADAM DAVIS BEATTY
ROYCE SHARP
MATT KENDRICK

PRODUCTION PHOTOS BY
SANDRA AND JOHN BENT

nethuen | drama

Methuen Drama

1 3 5 7 9 10 8 6 4 2

First published in 2012

Methuen Drama
Bloomsbury Publishing Plc
50 Bedford Square
London WC1B 3DP
www.methuendrama.com

Copyright © Rena Cook 2012

Rena Cook has asserted her rights under the Copyright, Designs and Patents Act, 1988, to be identified as the author of this work

A CIP catalogue record for this book is available from the British Library

PB ISBN: 978 1 408 15460 1
E PUB ISBN: 978 1 408 15714 5

Available in the USA from Bloomsbury Academic & Professional,
175 Fifth Avenue/3rd Floor, New York, NY 10010
www.BloomsburyAcademicUSA.com

Typeset by Country Setting, Kingsdown, Kent CT14 8ES
Printed and bound in Great Britain by Martins The Printers, Berwick-upon-Tweed

For Joe Mitcho

my husband and partner, who first encouraged me
to write and read every word of this book.

Acknowledgments

No one works in isolation; we are all products of the many generous individuals who come in and out of our lives. I am no exception. The content of this book is an amalgam of all the master voice teachers I have trained with through the years. Each time I walk into a classroom, I take them with me: David Carey, Jane Boston, Gillyanne Kayes, Rocco Dal Vera, Patsy Rodenburg, Kristin Linklater, Cecily Berry, Antonio Ocampo-Guzman, Judylee Vivier, Debbie Green, Morwenna Rowe, Louis Colaianni, Kelly McEvenue, Dudley Knight, Paul Meier and Rebecca Clark Carey.

I also want to thank my students at the University of Oklahoma who practiced this work with me and shared their thoughts that you will read as "Colin" and "Kristina". They are Colin Welch, Kristina Love, Kelcie Miles, Alli Trussell, Joel Behne, Morgen Reed and Courtney Kimbrough. To Anna Fearheiley, my student editorial assistant, special thanks for her eagle eye.

A large thank you also to my University of Oklahoma colleagues who provided support during the writing of this book: the Vice President for Research of the University of Oklahoma Weitzenhoffer Family College of Fine Arts, Dean Rich Taylor, School of Drama Director Tom Huston Orr, Dr Kae Koger and Rick Reeves.

Finally, thanks to Kim Moore, an extraordinary high school drama teacher, who taught with me in ranks thirty years ago. She was the one who said, "Yes, this book is needed." I believed her.

Contents

Preface for teachers

Voice and the Young Actor is a textbook whose mission is to demystify the speaking voice for the high-school drama student, or any student for that matter, who wants to use the voice more clearly, easily and expressively. Though the language of this book owes its origins to the world of theatrical performance, the same principles and processes will work for students involved in debate, forensics, speech tournaments and government. Through the course of this book, we will explore relaxation, natural alignment, breath, resonance, articulation, daily warm-ups, simple vocal anatomy and vocal health and safety. Our goal is to help young actors understand and celebrate their own voices and give them a process to free tensions and habits in order to discover the natural clarity, power and dynamics of their individual voices.

I was a high-school drama teacher myself for sixteen years, so I know first-hand the challenges you face with many high-school students who cannot be heard or understood from the stage. They are unaccustomed to opening the mouth when they speak and are culturally encouraged to trail off at the ends of sentences. They often use only the lowest notes of their pitch range. These usage issues are further reinforced by our society's current obsession with social media, texting and instant messages, which have become substitutes for face-to-face and voice-to-voice interaction. Young people, as a group, are losing the ability to use the voice effectively and expressively to communicate. It is in the realm of theatrical performance where this trend is most obvious.

It is my deep belief that voice work has tremendous value for students as actors and more importantly, at this age, as human beings. They are switched on about acting right now but we know that many of them will not pursue careers on the stage. However, the transformational process of vocal development will have rewards far beyond being able to hear your students in the last row of the auditorium. They will gain presence, confidence, vocal clarity and improved dynamic expressivity that will support them in whatever path they choose after high school or college.

In my travels as a college recruiter, an adjudicator for competitive theater, and a workshop presenter at Thespian conferences, I have been asked on numerous occasions, "How can I get my students to speak up, to be clear, to articulate, to use the voice in more healthy ways?" It is for this reason that I was encouraged to create *Voice and the Young Actor*. This book is for you and your students. It is designed as a journey that we will take together. Joining you on this journey are two real students, Colin and Kristina, who have worked through the entire vocal development sequence. Throughout the book, they share, in their blogs, responses and discoveries, sometimes even their frustrations, as they model for your students how to reflect on what they are learning. Verbal and written expressions of how the work is affecting them are crucial to deeper understandings and lasting vocal growth. Space is provided at the end of each chapter for reflective journaling.

Most of the narrative within this book is addressed to the students, like a dialogue that I am having with them about a subject for which I have great passion. The "Teacher Tips" sections are addressed to you with additional information that will help you guide your group through this book.

A crucial feature of this book and an essential to the philosophy of the process outlined here is an invitation to a variety of dialects and cultural backgrounds – all voices are welcome at the table. Exercises are included that encourage discussions of self-discovery and group inclusion. I understand that you might only have your students an hour a day and there is so much ground to cover in drama or speech class. I have designed the lessons so that they can be done as a whole voice unit or as parts of each class period. Regular voice work, as a cornerstone of your drama or speech curriculum, including daily vocal warm-ups is necessary for the true transformational outcomes that this process can produce.

The book is arranged sequentially. Chapter 2, "What are vocal folds anyway?" and Chapter 3, "Protecting the jewels", are placed early because they contain useful information to have as the students go through the rest of the sequence. However, I usually teach this information alongside activities in Chapters 4 and 5. Anatomy and voice care can be dry compared to the other, more active chapters. Use them in a way that feels organic and useful to your students without sacrificing the momentum of the more practical exercises.

Each of you, working together with your students, will find your own way through the material in this book and adapt it to the needs of the group and the time allotted to the study of voice. What follows, though, is a plan of study that some of you may find useful.

Begin each voice session with a comprehensive vocal and physical warm-up. You can create warm-ups from ideas presented in Chapter 13 or you can design your own by choosing one or two exercises from Chapters 4 to 9.

As I said, anatomy should come early; the paper larynx will take a whole class period. Vocal health can be touched on in several sessions. You will find yourself reinforcing these principles regularly, not only through voice sessions but in rehearsals, as the actors will need to be reminded frequently about voice care.

The primary content of each voice class will be found in Chapters 4 to 9. You can do a chapter a day, or if you have the luxury of time, two to three class periods per chapter.

The last fifteen minutes of each class could focus on the students' text work, which can be done as a group or coached individually with the rest of the group assisting in the explorations, as outlined in Chapters 11 and 12. Ideally you and your class would have time to do four performances related to their work on voice: a sonnet or monologue, the legend or fairy tale, the political speech, and the cultural voice assignment. These four text-based performances could be broken up in the following way:

○ Monologue or sonnet with Chapters 4 to 6.

○ Legend or fairy tale with Chapters 7 and 8.

○ Political speech with Chapters 11 and 12.

○ Cultural voice as part of a final performance or showcase.

I want to add a final note about the National Standards for Theater Education. We are all aware of the current need in our schools to focus curricula toward these standardized guidelines. As these guidelines are worded, *Voice and the Young Actor* meets content standard number two which states:

> Students in grades 9–12 should show proficiency in acting by developing, communicating and sustaining characters in improvisations and informal or formal productions.
>
> ○ **Achievement Standard:** analyze the physical, emotional and social dimensions of characters found in dramatic texts from various genre and media.
>
> ○ **Achievement Standard:** compare and demonstrate various classical and contemporary acting techniques and methods.
>
> ○ **Achievement Standard:** in an ensemble, create and sustain characters that communicate with audiences.

Voice and the Young Actor will aid students in gaining proficiency in clarity of vocal communication in both formal and informal productions. Particularly in the second half of the book, this process will help students move toward proficiency in physicalizing and emotionally embodying characters in dramatic texts. Further, the process outlined herein will open your actors to embrace vocally both classical and contemporary acting techniques. Finally, it will lead to proficiency in creating characters who communicate to audiences with clear, strong and expressive voices.

Through the years, my respect for teachers has grown and my belief that we are all changing the world through theater has not diminished. As my passion for voice has developed in the last decade, I stand firm in the belief that one of the greatest gifts we can give our students is a strong, clear voice, and *Voice and the Young Actor* takes us a step closer to that goal. I hope you will find this work as exciting, energetic and transformative as my students and I have found it. Trust yourself and go. The best way to learn new material is to teach it!

Preface for students

Colin's blog

First day of voice class: a little scary, have no idea what to expect. I know I need it, because my drama teacher says she can't hear me on stage. So I shout my lines and I end up with a sore throat. I can't win. I talk to my friends, and it's easy; they understand me just fine. My mother says I mumble. I think she is just hard of hearing.

Colin is expressing a frustration that you may share. We are all more casual about how we communicate these days. We don't even have to speak in full sentences; in fact we don't even have to use language at all. We text more than we speak; we post abbreviated thoughts in shorthand on Facebook. Why not? It's faster, easier and certainly more efficient; you can communicate with a lot more people at one time. Styles of communication have definitely changed. You and your friends can text with speed and efficiency; in seconds, you can keep up with friends and family all over the world. You are masters of the new communication technology! But if you want to get cast in the play, if you dream of playing the lead, it's all about the voice. Can you be heard? Can you be understood? Does your voice reflect the needs and feelings of the character you are playing?

Kristina's blog

I've always been proud of how I sound; my parents would always ask me to sing for their friends. I used to hide in the bathroom, and my dad would slip dollar bills under the door to get me to come out and sing for my grand-parents. But my director didn't cast me in the lead because she said I talk like a little girl. I speak too softly and I speak too slowly. When I try to change that, she says I am shouting and talking too fast. I don't get it.

Like Colin, Kristina may be sharing thoughts that you have experienced as well. You may also have been disappointed when the cast list went up and your name was not where you hoped it would be. You have discovered that being in a play is fun or winning the debate trophy is cool. Some of you know you want to be attorneys, teachers, preachers or sportscasters. I also venture to say that some of you may already know that acting is going to be your life's passion. If you are going to be a professional voice user in any arena, you have to begin to focus on your voice now. Are you loud enough? Are you clear enough? Are you vocally expressive so that your voice transforms into the character?

There are many reasons why the questions posed above can prove challenging to young actors. Culturally it is uncool to speak with a lot of expressivity, energy or passion; your friends may look at you like, "Wow, what's up with you?" We also carry our bodies in more relaxed and even "slouchy" ways. Sometimes it is to keep our oversized pants (which I know are totally cool) from sliding off our hips. Tall, willowy young women may be hiding the fact that their bodies are developing, and drooping shoulders make those changes less obvious. Perhaps you have gotten used to allowing the spine to collapse a little so you don't call attention to yourself. The current youth culture reinforces these and other habits that do not help you engage the voice in a larger context such as performing on the stage.

This book is all about voice. More accurately, it outlines a process for the development of an effective, healthy and expressive voice that will serve you on the stage and beyond. We will learn that our "habitual alignment" actually inhibits our ability to speak loudly and clearly and that "natural alignment" lets the voice move more efficiently.

Another vocal habit that we inherit from our culture is "falling inflection disease", which is rampant in American English. Dropping volume and pitch at the ends of sentences is a widespread habit that doesn't serve the actor (or any communicator for that matter) well. We will discover through our work together that it is a pretty easy habit to eliminate with a little time and focused attention.

Also through our work we will learn the importance of deep central breathing to the production of sound: for volume, clarity and vocal ease. Even more important, we will discover the role of the breath in keeping us calm and grounded, allowing us to connect to our own unique creative spark.

Some simple vocal anatomy will help us to understand how vocal sounds are produced, how flexible the vocal tract is, and how it contributes to resonance which gives each of us our unique sound or voice quality.

We will learn about all the wonderful sounds that the mouth can make. By creating more space in that mouth and finding more energy in the articulators, we can make clearer, richer sounds that communicate a wider range of characters and emotions – a great thing if your goal is to get cast.

Finally, we will learn how to carry our vocal process into acting. We will understand that voice work is not just a quick warm-up before a rehearsal; rather it provides the foundation for honest, clear and transformational performances.

This book contains a series of exercises and activities that will help you begin to explore and expand all the wonderful vocal possibilities that each of you possesses. If you work diligently and regularly, you will be able to speak loudly and clearly, with emotional connection and character transformation, in a healthy way that will not leave you with a sore throat at the end of a long rehearsal. Colin and Kristina will be taking the journey with you, sharing their thoughts, observations and discoveries in their blogs.

And me? I'm Rena, and I will be your guide. I started my theater career as an actor, but soon found that my first love was teaching. I taught high-school drama in Arizona and Oklahoma for sixteen years before I moved to teaching voice in university. In the last ten years I have taught thousands of young actors how to use their voices. Those students are now professional actors in television, movies, regional theater and Broadway. Many are also lawyers, teachers, agents, principals and political leaders. The process described in *Voice and the Young Actor* is transformational: it will affect not only your work on stage but in every other area of your life. Clear and dynamic verbal communication is the centerpiece of success in all areas of our lives, whether personal, theatrical or professional.

Voice and the young actor

1 I hate my voice

Before we begin actual work on our voice, let's get to know and understand our own voices a little better. When I ask students to describe their voices, often I hear this: "I hate my voice! When I hear it on a recording, I can't believe I sound like that." We are all surprised when we hear our own voices for the first time. We are used to hearing and sensing our voices from the inside out; we have a completely different experience of our voices than the rest of the world does. Aspects of our voice may be amplified to us and ring in our ears: "I never thought I sounded that high pitched," "I sound like my mom!" or "My voice is so nasal." We may also have judgment attached to our perceptions which can make us feel vulnerable, shy and even a little defensive when our voice is under examination. We instinctively feel a very personal connection to the way our voice sounds.

The truth is, our speaking voice is both personal and public. It is connected to the core of who we are. It is linked to our past, our upbringing, our emotions, our motivations and desires, and to our health. Our voice reveals to the world who we really are. Whether we are confident, secure, happy, healthy, inspired or intimidated, our voice tells all. People make judgments about us as soon as we open our mouths, as soon as we utter a word. We are found to be intelligent or not, mature or not, confident or not, castable or not, hirable or not, believable or not. These assumptions are often formed solely on the quality of our voice and the clarity of our speech.

It is no secret that desire and sincerity alone are not enough these days to get you where you want to go. Talent and hard work may not be enough to get cast in the show, to be hired for the job or to convince your parents and teachers that you are worthy of trust. The impact you make on others in school, at home, in the workplace, among your friends or on stage is a combination of personal qualities that affects not only what you say but how you say it. No personal quality speaks louder than the voice. An individual's ability to use the voice in an expressive, open, relaxed, clear and articulate manner is a tool for success in virtually any area of modern life. A skillfully used, dynamic and expressive voice will serve you in auditions, interviews, in the classroom – even at parties.

How often are desire, talent, intelligence and sincerity trapped inside a voice that does not communicate the true essence of a person? A nasal quality or a strident sound can be annoying and off-putting. A monotonous sound can disengage an audience within a sentence or two. A weak voice, unsupported by breath, lacks a sense of sincerity and cannot rouse an audience to buy into the character.

Understand that you are not the only one who has been embarrassed or teased about the way you sound. For boys, the voice change may have been a period of awkward squawking and abrupt and uncontrollable pitch changes as vocal folds recalibrated into manhood. For girls, the voice may still retain the high pitch and shrill quality of early childhood, and staying "Daddy's little girl" may feel safe and comfortable. Or you may have been told so many times to use your "inside voice" that your strong voice has gone into hiding and you now can only speak softly. Conversely, if you were the baby of a large family you may have learned to shout to be heard, and now people cover their ears when you approach. Whatever vocal habit we picked up along the road to maturity, there was generally merciless teasing involved, from our own families or other children in the neighborhood. So there are all sorts of reasons why we, at this point in our vocal development, "hate our voices".

Self-image also plays significantly into how much we accept or reject our voices. As young actors we are still sorting out what kind of person we are going to be. Our thoughts of self change almost daily with positive reinforcement, negative feedback, successes or perceived failures. Our family of origin and the cultural influences we have experienced affect how we use our voices, and expectations or pressure from parents, siblings or peers all have impact on how we sound and speak. If you speak English with a dialect, you may be proud of where you come from or you may have been made to feel ashamed for being different.

Wherever your voice is today, whatever factors make up the way you use speech, volume, pitch and quality, it is within your control, and you always have the right to choose what you want to keep, what you want to set aside and how you want to develop. My job is to help you become aware of the options available to you as you come to understand how the voice works.

Let's look at the controllable properties of the voice:

Quality Sometimes called tone, quality is the unique sound that each voice has, how we recognize one voice from another. Some words we might use to describe a person's quality are: pleasing, warm, resonant, soothing, raspy, nasal, deep, dark, plummy.

Volume The relative loudness or softness of the voice, which should change according to the needs of the situation. "How do I increase my volume?" and "How can I get my actors to speak louder?" are the two most frequently asked questions that I get when conducting workshops. When on stage we may need to be loud, to shout over crowd noise without damaging our voice. Or we may want to speak softly while still being heard in the back row. We will learn that breath and resonance are the master keys to your volume control.

Pitch The highness or lowness of the voice. We often get trapped into one or two notes of pitch variation, when in actuality we could have two octaves at our disposal. For actors, pitch flexibility is the goal, and to that end expanding and extending pitch range gets a whole chapter of its own in this book.

Inflection   The movement of the pitch through a phrase, sentence or groups of sentences. For example, a monotone speaker has a flat inflection pattern with no pitch variation – every note is the same. An Irish speaker will have a very different inflection pattern from a General American speaker. The actor who can use inflection variety will be a better storyteller, will be better able to communicate dense lines of text to an audience in a clear and compelling way.

Tempo   How fast or how slowly you speak. Ideally you want to be able to use a variety of tempos. Often we get stuck in a rhythm that becomes our default tempo, and this can either be too fast or too slow. As with volume and inflection, we want to develop flexibility so we can use a variety of tempos to give us a full range of expression.

All of these vocal properties are within your control! It does take practice, but as you work through the exercises in this book you will find that the quality, volume, pitch, inflection and tempo of your voice will all develop ease and flexibility. What every actor wants, right!

Exercises

In order to understand our own voices in more detail, finish the following sentences in the space provided below (example: I hope I don't sound "like a little girl", "squeaky", "too butch", "like a hick" or "like an airhead". I hope I do sound "sexy", "masculine", "confident" or "friendly"). Think of several responses to each question – don't settle for the first easy answer.

I hope I don't sound like

I hope I do sound like

The voices I most like to listen to are

The voices that I find most annoying to listen to sound like

The feedback I often get on my voice is

What I like best about my voice is

My vocal challenges are

Goals for my vocal development include

For class discussion

Voices from heaven – voices from hell

- What celebrities have voices from heaven? What qualities do these voices have that earn that designation?

- What celebrities have voices from hell? What qualities do these voices have that earn that designation?

- What kind of voice compels you to listen or draws you in? What kind of voice turns you off or shuts you down?

Teacher tip

The following class assignment is a great exercise to encourage the students to think more deeply about why their voices sound as they do and what factors contributed to their vocal development. It also encourages them to talk about family background and dialects they may have. It is important to stress that dialect is not a disability to be gotten rid of, but a neutral fact that is an important part of who one is. All sounds, dialects and voice qualities are acceptable. Our goal in voice study is to learn, through practice, to be clear and emotionally connected to spontaneous impulse. We also want to develop flexibility to adapt to whatever dialect or vocal quality the role requires while maintaining vocal health and safety.

My personal voice house

Purposes of this assignment

1 To give you time to reflect on how you sound right now and an opportunity to examine what factors have shaped your "personal voice house".

2 To celebrate the diversity and uniqueness of each individual voice. There is no good voice or bad voice, no right dialect or wrong dialect.

The assignment

Create a collage of pictures that reveals, in picture form, how your voice has developed. What are the factors, people and events that have shaped how you sound, what words you use, and your dialect? What are your vocal challenges and your vocal strengths?

Gather pictures and artfully display them on poster board or cardboard. These pictures can be family photos, collected from magazines, even hand-drawn or computer-generated images. Each should depict some aspect of your vocal development, your "personal voice house". For example, if you have a dialect, show a picture from the region or country or a picture of the person (actual or symbolic representation) who has influenced your sound.

Other questions that might spark your imagination:

○ *Where were you born?*

○ *What type of family did you grow up in?*

○ *Do you now or have you ever smoked?*

○ *What is your family birth order?*

○ *What language was spoken in your home as you grew up? Do you, your parents or your friends speak English with a dialect?*

○ *Were you Daddy's girl, or did you have big brothers that inspired a "macho" sound?*

○ *Did you grow up in a large city with a diverse ethnic population or in the rural countryside?*

○ *Have you received consistent feedback on your voice?*

○ *Did you wear braces or have an illness or injury that affected your voice?*

○ *What musical instrument do you sound like?*

○ *What are your vocal goals?*

Share your "personal voice house" collage

You will have three minutes to share your collage with the class and discuss why you chose the pictures you did.

Suggested grading criteria

1 Detail and depth of your examination of how you sound and why.

2 Creativity of display.

3 Focused and polished presentation.

Kristina's blog

Many of my classmates shared personal stories about why they speak and behave as they do – whether the reason was to emulate someone they admired or specifically not sound like someone that they grew up around. I was absolutely shocked by how much I learned by listening to everyone else. I also found it fascinating where everyone comes from – it does help you to understand people more. It was funny to hear how some people talked about not having an accent while at the same time displaying a very deep one. It makes me curious if I share that delusion. Maybe we all have accents.

Colin's blog

I was born in Boston, then moved to Texas when I was ten, so I've grown up hearing two totally different dialects. I hope I don't sound like I'm from Texas and I try not to let the Boston accent creep in there. I strive to sound professional, mature and manly. I don't want my voice to hold me back from getting roles. This class is going to be about discovering myself. I am excited to break bad habits, challenge my voice and become a better actor and person.

Reflective voice blog

Purpose of this assignment

To promote your ability to reflect critically on your vocal development.

The assignment

I suggest that you keep a reflective voice blog for each class period that you do voice work. You can write in the spaces provided at the end of each chapter, or you can keep a separate folder or diary. The blog should be more than a narrative of what was done each day in class. It should also focus on your personal reflections on the work: what you learned, realized, were confused about, didn't feel successful with, exercises that worked especially well, ideas to incorporate in your personal warm-up, or breakthroughs. In short, you want to monitor your progress regarding your own vocal discoveries and development. You will also want to observe in your blog the group-learning process, which is how your classmates contributed to your learning.

Teacher tip

The blog can be read and evaluated in any way you choose. What follows is the process I find useful. The blog is evaluated twice during the semester: at mid-term and at the end of the semester. It is worth a total of 100 points toward the final grade, 50 points each time it is graded. In order to get 90–100 points, a blog entry must be written for each class and be more than a narrative of what happened. It should include (1) a statement of how the group contributed to their learning that day, (2) a discovery that they made, or something new they learned, (3) a question that they might have asked themselves, or one that was clarified, (4) a point that they want to remember and include in their personal process.

Reflective voice blog

How has your understanding of your own voice changed? What new vocal goals have you set? How did listening to the other students in the class affect your understanding of how voice habits develop?

Teacher tip

Before discussing the contents of Chapter 1, you may want to lead the class in a vocal warm-up. It will not only get the group thinking about components of voice work, but will also allow them to experience how good a warmed-up voice can sound and feel. In addition, a warm-up will focus the body, mind and voice to be ready and open for what is to follow. Look at Chapter 13 for warm-up suggestions.

Chapter 1 references

For more information on the topics discussed in this chapter refer to:

Barton, Robert, and Dal Vera, Rocco, *Voice Onstage and Off*, 2nd edn. New York and Oxford: Routledge, 2011.

Linklater, Kristin, *Freeing the Natural Voice*. Hollywood: Drama Publishers, 2006.

Rodenburg, Patsy, *The Right to Speak*. New York: Routledge, 1992.

2 What are vocal folds anyway?

What are the vocal folds anyway? Where are they? How do they work? How do I know when I am hurting them? Why do I seem always to get sick just before a show opens? After I cheer at a football game I have no voice at all – what's that about? Any of these questions sound familiar to you?

For many voice users, including many professional actors and singers, the voice is a mystery. Sometimes it works; sometimes it doesn't. Sometimes the sound is all there and it feels great; sometimes it sounds hoarse, husky and thin, beyond our conscious control. What I want to do in this chapter is remove the veil of mystery from the voice. It can be understood, taken care of and used in such a way that it is predictable and reliable. The voice should serve you, not the other way around.

We will start with some basic vocal anatomy. You need to know what's in there, what the major parts are, how they work, how to develop them, and how to care for them.

The key terminology in vocal anatomy

Vocal folds: the sound source – two flaps of tissue with a layer of muscle at the core, attached to cartilages in the larynx. Their oscillation, or opening and closing against the air stream, creates the sound we call voice.

Larynx: commonly known as the voice box, the larynx houses and protects the vocal folds. The Adam's apple is the most visible part of the larynx.

Glottis: the opening or space between the vocal folds.

Subglottal pressure: the buildup of air pressure below the closed vocal folds which causes the folds to blow open and subsequently snap back shut, creating tiny puffs of air that we ultimately hear as voice.

Epiglottis: a leaf-shaped structure that folds down over the vocal folds to protect the airways when we swallow food or water. It is lifted when we speak or sing.

Hyoid: horseshoe-shaped bone above the larynx, the only free-floating bone in the body. It connects the larynx to structures above and below.

Thyroid: shield-shaped cartilage providing front protection for the vocal folds. It is flexible, like the visor of a knight's helmet.

Cricoid: shaped like a signet ring, the cricoid sits at the bottom of the larynx, providing foundation and stability.

Arytenoids: two pyramid-shaped cartilages that sit on top of the cricoids, behind the thyroid, connecting to the vocal folds. They are responsible for opening and closing the vocal folds and lengthening and bunching the vocal folds: movements associated with pitch changes.

Extrinsic muscles: large strap muscles that raise and lower the larynx.

Intrinsic muscles: these move the cartilages of the larynx, and because the vocal folds are attached to the cartilages the vocal folds move when the cartilages move.

Diaphragm: a large dome-shaped muscle that sits under the lungs and on top of the stomach. It bisects the entire torso, and contracts and moves down on the inhale, allowing the lungs to fill with air.

How these structures fit and work together to make sound

The **larynx** is a structure in the throat that houses the vocal folds. You can feel it by finding your Adam's apple with your middle finger and placing the adjacent fingers above and below it. Swallow and feel the entire larynx move up and down. Yawn and feel the larynx move down. That whole moveable bit is the larynx. It is made of one bone – the hyoid; and three cartilages – the thyroid, the cricoid and the arytenoids.

The **hyoid** bone is at the very top of the larynx. You can feel your hyoid by placing your hand under your jaw and at the top of your throat. If that is not clear, place your finger in

THE LARYNX - FRONT

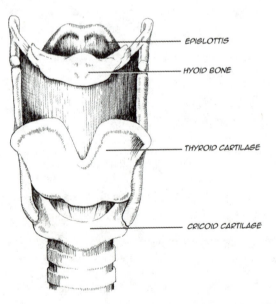

EPIGLOTTIS

HYOID BONE

THYROID CARTILAGE

CRICOID CARTILAGE

THE LARYNX - BACK

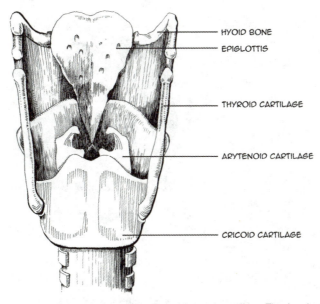

- HYOID BONE
- EPIGLOTTIS
- THYROID CARTILAGE
- ARYTENOID CARTILAGE
- CRICOID CARTILAGE

the center at the very top of your throat, raise your chin and swallow. The hard, moving bit there is the hyoid bone. It is not directly connected to any other bone, making it the only free-floating bone in the body. It provides protection and stability to the top of the larynx. Muscles connect the hyoid to the base of the skull, the jaw, sternum and collarbone.

The **thyroid** cartilage is larger in front and opens to the back. It is shaped like a shield. The Adam's apple, or vocal notch, is part of the thyroid. It is more prominent in men than in women because the male vocal folds are longer, making the thyroid longer back to front. Its function is protection, stability and flexibility. It has the capacity to move up and down like the face guard on a knight's helmet.

The **cricoid** cartilage provides the bottom layer, or foundation, of the larynx. It is shaped like a signet ring: larger in the back than in front. You can feel the cricoid by placing the middle finger again on the Adam's apple; lifting the chin slightly, with your next finger below, you feel a slight indentation, and below that you should feel another little ridge – that is your cricoid.

The **arytenoids** are, in my opinion, the most interesting, as their shape is so unique and their function so complex and important to actual creation of sound and pitch variety. The arytenoids are a matched set of two cartilages shaped like pyramids. They sit at the back of the thyroid, on top of the cricoid. It is the movement of the arytenoids which is responsible for opening and closing the vocal folds.

VOCAL FOLDS - OPEN

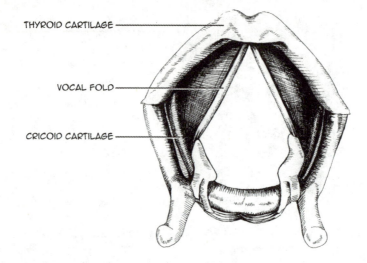

THYROID CARTILAGE ————

VOCAL FOLD ————

CRICOID CARTILAGE ————

How we make sound

As interesting as all these structures are, it is even more interesting to understand how they work together to create sound. First, the brain sends a signal that it wishes to speak. The diaphragm contracts and moves down, creating negative pressure in the torso, which causes air to rush into the lungs. When air pressure in the lungs is sufficient, the diaphragm relaxes and moves back up, and abdominal muscles manage the outgoing air flow.

VOCAL FOLDS - CLOSED

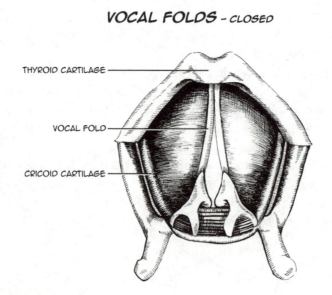

THYROID CARTILAGE ————

VOCAL FOLD ————

CRICOID CARTILAGE ————

Subglottal pressure builds up under the closed vocal folds. When air pressure is sufficient, the vocal folds blow open. This creates negative pressure in the glottis, which causes the vocal folds to snap shut again. This blowing open and snapping shut happens hundreds of times per second, creating tiny puffs of air which sound a little like quacks. These puffs of disturbed air move to the resonating chambers of the throat, mouth and nasal cavities, where they are amplified and enriched. The articulators then turn this sound into intelligible speech. What an amazing process!

Activity: build a paper larynx

Teacher tip

This is an excellent way to learn the parts of the larynx and see in three dimensions how they fit together and which parts have flexibility and which are stationary. This paper model is given to us courtesy of Gillyanne Kayes and Jeremy Fisher at Vocal Process, www.vocalprocess.co.uk. You will need a pair of scissors, a glue stick, and small brass brads to make your mobile paper larynx. If each student has their own scissors it takes about twenty minutes. If you share scissors, plan on forty minutes for all to complete. You will find it is well worth the time. Follow the instructions overleaf.

Colin's blog

Before this class I never even thought about my larynx, let alone crafted one! Rena gave all of us scissors, a glue stick, some brads, and shapes to cut out. In just a few minutes I created a paper larynx. Who knew this mechanism was made up of three cartilages? I also learned there are two sets of muscles – the extrinsic and the intrinsic – and the vocal folds themselves are five layers deep. It is insanely amazing to think that such small parts of our bodies do so many important things.

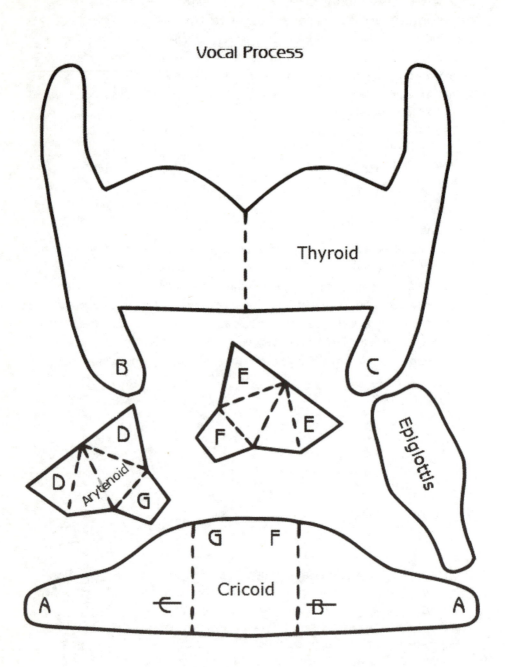

Vocal Process

Thyroid

B

C

E

E

F

D

D

Arytenoid

G

Epiglottis

G

F

A

Cricoid

B

A

Build Your Own Tilting Larynx: Instructions

You will need: One paper template
Scissors
Glue
4 small paper fasteners

Preparation

1. Cut around the thick outlines of the **thyroid cartilage** and the **cricoid cartilage,** the **two arytenoids** and **the epiglottis.**
2. Fold along the dotted lines
3. Make a small horizontal cut along the thick lines through the letters B and C on the cricoid cartilage.

Gluing
Cricoid cartilage

4. Glue the cricoid cartilage to make a complete "ring" (glue one A on top of the other). The letters should be on the outside of the ring.

Arytenoid cartilages

5. Glue the first arytenoid cartilage to form a three-sided pyramid (glue face D on top of the other face D). Leave the rectangular flap at the bottom free.
6. Repeat with the other arytenoids cartilage, gluing face E on top of the other face E.

Building the larynx with the paper fasteners
Arytenoid cartilages to Cricoid cartilage

7. Join the first arytenoid cartilage onto the cricoid cartilage, using a paper fastener. Line the F flap up on the outside of the cricoid "ring", with the arytenoid pyramid overhanging inside. Then secure with a paper fastener, pushing through flap F on the arytenoids cartilage and point F on the cricoid cartilage, and opening the fastener up inside the ring to secure it.
8. Repeat with the second arytenoid and paper fastener, lining up the G flap with point G on the cricoid "ring". Both pyramids should overhang inside the ring and above it.

Cricoid cartilage to Thyroid cartilage

9. Join the thyroid cartilage to the cricoid cartilage, using the remaining two paper fasteners. Line up point B on the thyroid cartilage to point B on the cricoid cartilage. The thyroid should be outside the cricoid "ring" with the long arms pointing up above the arytenoids.
   Push the paper fastener through point B on the thyroid cartilage, and through the slot you cut earlier on point B of the cricoid "ring". Open the fastener to secure it.
10. Repeat with point C on the thyroid cartilage, securing it with the paper fastener through the slot at point C on the cricoid "ring". The thyroid cartilage should sit outside the cricoid "ring", with the folded "notch" overhanging the joined narrow section of the ring.

Epiglottis to Thyroid cartilage (optional)

11. The narrow tip of the epiglottis glues onto the inside of the thyroid cartilage, approximately two thirds of the way down. The body of the epiglottis then sits up above the thyroid notch.

Reflective voice blog

How has your understanding of vocal anatomy changed? What is clearer to you than before? What do you still have questions about?

Chapter 2 references

For more information on the topics discussed in this chapter, refer to:

Bunch, Meribeth, *The Dynamics of the Singing Voice*, 4th edn. New York: SpringerWein, 1997.

Carey, David, and Clark Carey, Rebecca, *Vocal Arts Workbook and DVD*. London: Methuen Drama, 2008.

DeVore, Kate, and Cookman, Starr, *The Voice Book*. Chicago: Chicago Review Press, 2009.

Kayes, Gillyanne, *Singing and the Actor*, 2nd edn. London: A & C Black, 2004.

Linklater, Kristin, *Freeing the Natural Voice*. Hollywood: Drama Publishers, 2006.

3 Protecting the jewels

You only get one voice in your life. If it breaks, you can't go out and buy a new one. So you must know how to care for it to ensure that it lasts a lifetime. You now need to learn to "protect the jewels", those two delicate vocal folds that are about the size of your thumbnails. Make no mistake, keeping your voice healthy is under your control and it is your responsibility. How your voice feels and functions is not a matter of chance or genetics, but of conscious choice and daily attention. If you make large demands on your voice, you should be aware of what the voice needs to stay healthy.

Now, before you dive into this long list of do's and don'ts, I know that you are not a monk; I know you have a life to live and not every moment can be spent worrying about your voice. But if you want to be an actor, singer, broadcaster, lawyer or anyone who uses their voice to make a living, you have to start being aware of the things that can damage your instrument. Here are a few strategies that can keep it healthy.

Get plenty of rest

Boy, this is a hard one. There are so many things we have to get done in a day, and sleep just isn't as important as getting that paper finished, talking on the phone to your best friend, or playing one more video game. The voice is one of the first parts of the body to feel fatigue and the last to feel rested. We live in a society that remains sleep-deprived much of the time. We expect our bodies to perform at high levels, often with insufficient rest. However, if you want your voice to be in the best shape possible on opening night, both body and voice need to be well rested.

In addition to rest at night, your voice needs periods of quiet throughout the day, particularly if you are a heavy voice user. I talk to my students in terms of "vocal units". This is a metaphor for thinking about the endurance capacity that a voice has throughout any given day. For example, let's say that you have ten vocal units available to you each day. You may use three units in the morning as you shout at your brother to get out of the bathroom. You may use three more vocal units at school as you holler at your friend in a noisy hall by your locker. And another three may be spent cheering at sports events. Then, if you have a three-hour rehearsal, you only have one unit left for a task that may require four. If you must use your voice beyond its daily unit allotment, the voice will begin to show fatigue. It may not be as loud, it may sound a bit husky, or you may feel a thickness in the larynx. For your voice, a little quiet time with a cup of warm tea can feel like a rest.

Budgeting vocal units is a very important aspect of maintaining good vocal health. If you know that the greatest demands on your voice will be made at a 7 p.m. rehearsal, then you should start conserving vocal units for the period of highest need. Each person's vocal units are different. Some people have voices of steel with a seemingly endless supply of vocal units. These fortunate few seem to be able to use, and even abuse, the voice for long periods of time without any negative effects. Others may feel fatigue after a lengthy conversation on the phone. You can increase your vocal units with proper usage, thinking about length in the back of the neck and using adequate breath support. But the fact that your voice has just so much it can give you in a day is a reality that must be honored if you want to keep it healthy.

When you are not rested and the voice is tired from overuse, you are also more susceptible to colds and flu. Tired vocal folds are irritated, inflamed and swollen, making them highly susceptible to germs. To stay healthy, stay rested.

Drink plenty of water

Water keeps the vocal folds hydrated, which is very important in maintaining general vocal health. Eight glasses of water a day is a good rough figure. My students get used to carrying a bottle of water with them all the time. Be especially diligent about hydration both before and after a demanding rehearsal or performance. A good rule of thumb is: you know you are well hydrated if you pee pale.

Avoid caffeine, carbonated beverages, acidic juices, milk and alcohol

This is particularly true before heavy voice usage. Caffeine and alcohol are diuretics, draining moisture from the body and more specifically from the vocal folds, and milk causes an increase in phlegm, which can lead to the need to clear the throat. It feels to me that carbonated beverages strip natural moisture from the throat and create gas in the stomach, which can surprise an actor in embarrassing ways. Acidic juices can irritate the stomach, causing reflux that irritates the vocal folds. Not all people react in the same way to these beverages. You need to know your voice and give it what it needs to operate at optimal efficiency. When in doubt, drink water or warm herbal tea and lots of it.

Avoid talking in competition with loud noises: in subway stations or airplanes, at noisy parties or near loud music

Talking over noise causes our vocal folds to work harder. We do it unconsciously. My recommendation is, if possible, to avoid using the voice in these situations. When it is not possible, be sure that you are using deep central breathing and keeping a long back of neck. Social chitchat and talking on the phone can be great vocal unit drainers as well. Think about the alignment you assume when talking on the phone – most of us literally let the body cave in on itself. Effort goes right to the vocal folds and stays there.

Don't smoke

Cigarette smoking causes all kinds of health problems, including heart disease, stroke, cancer, high blood pressure, and premature aging of the skin. Cigarettes also have a profoundly negative effect on the voice. A nationally known voice coach, Jan Gist, says that smoking is like cooking the vocal folds. They stay constantly inflamed and more susceptible to hemorrhage, infection and swelling. Over time the smoker's voice gets husky and hoarse, and pitch range diminishes as the vocal folds lose elasticity. Second-hand smoke is equally hard on the voice. If you do smoke, get help to quit; it is a powerful addiction. If you don't smoke, don't start. Don't even try it. Studies show that an adolescent can become addicted to cigarettes within a single pack!

Avoid screaming

I call screaming a vocal marathon event. When an actor is required to scream onstage, she trains as if running a marathon, building up to it with warm-ups, cooling down afterwards, and resting for a time before engaging in the scream again. No matter how well trained the speaker, screaming cannot be done repeatedly without taking a vocal toll.

Athletic events and shouting to friends over loud music are two situations where screaming is common. With adequate breath support, length in the back of the neck and space in the mouth, you should be able to project the voice at a level that allows you to enjoy the game or be heard by your friends without severe laryngitis the next day.

Avoid pushing forward with the head and neck while speaking

It is common for us to extend the head and neck as we speak, particularly if we are intent on making a point. This postural habit, however, shortens the space in the back of the neck, raises the tension level in jaw and tongue, and cuts off the ability to access deep breathing. In both social and professional settings, I can improve my voice usage immediately by keeping length in the back of my neck and breathing a little more consciously and deeply.

Be aware of certain medications

Antihistamines, which you might take for allergies, can be drying. Be sure to drink more water while taking these medications. Avoid throat sprays that numb pain, since they can make vocal folds more susceptible to strain, infection or irritation. Mentholated lozenges are drying to the vocal folds – find non-mentholated substitutes.

Don't suck that lemon

An old remedy, sucking on lemons, still makes the rounds. Lemon is acidic and strips the throat of natural moisture (also bad for teeth enamel). You can add a little to your tea if that is comforting, but never drink it straight.

Take care of acid reflux

Acid reflux (which you may know as heartburn or indigestion) can bubble up and irritate the vocal folds, causing you to sound hoarse or husky. If you have regular bouts of heartburn, try to avoid eating heavy, fatty or spicy foods before bedtime. If it is a serious problem for you, a doctor can prescribe an acid blocker.

Don't clear your throat

That's a hard one, right? Most of us clear our throats quite often, to get rid of phlegm. But imagine just smacking your vocal folds together as hard as you can – that's what clearing the throat is. Sometimes you can drink some water to move the mucus around, or you can cough silently, or swallow, or blow air through your folds. If you must clear the throat, do it as gently and as infrequently as possible.

Speak at optimum pitch

Optimum pitch is the note around which our voice is the clearest and most efficient. Many of us speak below our optimum pitch. This tires the voice pretty quickly, especially if we are trying to project. Remember to "pitch up". See Chapter 8 for more information about optimum pitch.

A great resource on how to care for your voice is a book entitled *How to Take Care of Your Voice: The Lifestyle Guide for Singers and Talkers* by Joanna Cazden. The more you know, the better equipped you will be to keep your voice healthy for life.

Exercise

Complete, or comment on, the following:

In regards to taking care of my voice, what I already do pretty well is

A couple of things I could do better are

What surprised me about taking care of my voice is

Who do you know who has a lot of vocal stamina? How do you compare?

What two things are you going to try to remember every day regarding vocal health and safety?

Take a moment to find long back of neck, feel yourself sitting a little straighter in your chair, let a deep breath drop into your center, and feel a big space opening in the back of your throat. Let your body get familiar with this position of readiness. Your body is ready to support almost any social vocal demand: talking on the phone, telling a story to a group of friends, projecting over music, or leading a cheer.

Most frequently asked questions about the voice and voice care

Why do I always seem to get a cold right before a show opens?

Throughout rehearsals you have been using your voice pretty hard, rehearsing each night, maybe attending a football game or party, and your voice is tired. During tech week, when rehearsals run longer, you get even less rest. When the vocal folds are fatigued they swell and inflame to become a perfect place for viruses, which are in our environment all the time, to find a home. And you get sick just when you want most to be healthy. Remedy: get rest, eat as healthily as you can, drink lots of water, lessen your social voice usage, don't hug fellow actors or share drinks and food, and sanitize your hands often.

How do I know if I have vocal fatigue?

The first sign may be a thick feeling in the throat, or you may feel the need to clear the throat more often (the tired voice produces more mucus to protect itself). If it feels scratchy and you're not getting a cold, it is a sure sign that you have been abusing the voice. If you have been doing a lot of speaking or singing, the muscles may feel a bit achy. That is OK – but it does mean that you should rest the voice a bit. If it feels scratchy that is not OK, and you should stop what you are doing, drink water and rest. Sometimes a tired voice begins to sound weak; it may fall back to the bottom of the range, or notes in your pitch range which are normally easy may be creaky or disappear. That is not the time to push through. If you absolutely can't stop at the moment, make sure you are using breath support, keeping the back of the neck long, making space in the mouth and articulating clearly. All these actions will take pressure off your vocal folds. Oh, and (did I say?) drink water.

I have to shout on stage. Can that hurt my voice?

As I have said, shouting on stage is like a vocal marathon. It does take a toll, even if you are well trained. Do a good vocal warm-up before each session, drink plenty of water both before and after. Remember to breathe deeply, keep a long back of neck, space in the mouth, aim resonance at the roof of the mouth. Do a cool-down after a session of extended vocal use, which includes gentle sounding in the middle of your range, yawning and stretching followed by a large glass of water or some warm tea. Even the strongest voices cannot shout repeatedly. Sometimes a director wants to go over and over a scene of high intensity. It is OK to let the director know, "I have so many full screams left. Tell me when you would like me to use them." You are in charge of your vocal health; the director does not know what your limitations are. I am not recommending that you be a vocal diva, but I do encourage you to be your own vocal advocate and be clear about when you are hurting yourself or are in danger of hurting yourself.

What is laryngitis?

Laryngitis is swelling in the vocal folds so severe that they stop being able to vibrate at all, which means they cannot produce sound. It can be caused by a viral infection or by extreme overuse. In either case, don't use the voice or try to force sound. You risk permanent damage. Vocal rest for three days should help, but see a doctor to determine the cause. Anti-inflammatory medication like cortisone can be helpful in severe cases when you absolutely have to perform. Cortisone is an amazing but nasty drug, and should only be used when absolutely necessary. If you get laryngitis several times a year, you need to see an Ear, Nose and Throat doctor to find out what is going on – if it is a chronic physical condition or a functional issue related to long-term vocal misuse. In a case of long-term poor usage habits, speech therapists can be great resources. If you are going to be earning your living with your voice, you need to care for it and learn to use it correctly, and it is never too early to start.

What about the dreaded nodes? How do they happen? How should they be treated if it is determined that I have them?

Nodes or vocal nodules are like calluses on the vocal folds. An ENT or otolaryngologist can diagnose whether or not you have nodes by looking at your folds through a laryngoscope. They occur from repeated misuse, usually over a period of time. Cheerleaders, singers or actors who push the voice too hard are susceptible to nodes. If you are hoarse or sound husky for a long period of time or if you have lost notes in your pitch range, it's possible that nodes could be the culprit. They can go away by themselves, but only if the vocal abuse habit that caused them is eliminated. They can also be surgically removed. A good voice teacher or a speech pathologist can help you work out a healthy vocal regimen that can put you on the road to recovery. However, if the bad vocal behaviors recur, so will the nodes. A diagnosis of nodes is not the end of the road for an actor or singer, but it does signal that big changes need to take place if you are going to get your voice back in top condition. We have said it before, but it bears repeating: do a good vocal warm-up before you use your voice, drink plenty of water, maintain natural alignment, support the voice with deep breathing, keep the back of the neck long, make more space in the mouth, use the articulators, and don't push from the vocal folds.

Chapter 3 references

For more information on the topics discussed in this chapter refer to:

Cazden, Joanna, *How to Take Care of Your Voice: The Lifestyle Guide for Singers and Talkers*. Bangor: www.Booklocker.com, 2008.

Davies, D. Garfield, *Care of the Professional Voice: A Guide to Voice Management for Singers, Actors and Professional Voice Users*. New York: Routledge, 2005.

DeVore, Kate, and Cookman, Starr, *The Voice Book*. Chicago: Chicago Review Press, 2009.

4 Why am I so tense?

We are all familiar with tension. Tension is the inevitable by-product of living in a modern world. Tension is also the enemy of the expressive voice. Tension, anywhere in the body, stifles sound and muffles articulation. Learning how to release tension, then, is one of the first steps toward releasing a free, clear and dynamic voice. Releasing tension – that is, achieving a more relaxed state – is not to be confused with the relaxation that happens before sleep. We don't want to be limp noodles or rag dolls. We want to find a state of "relaxed readiness". Through the exercises outlined in this chapter, unnecessary tension is released so the body can energize and be ready for speech. Effective voice usage takes energy and focus and can only be accomplished from a starting point of release and relaxation.

The tension we normally carry in our bodies makes itself known in many insidious ways. These can include headaches, indigestion, muscle aches, joint pain, insomnia and free-floating anxiety. We are aware of the physical toll that stress and tension create, but most of us are unaware of the price we pay in our voices. The vocal folds, which actually produce the sound, are small, delicate membranes in the larynx. The weight of any tension in the body eventually radiates and finds its way to the folds, causing them to work harder than they should. Toes gripping the floor, knees that lock, a fixed pelvic girdle, a rigid spine, and tense arms, fingers, shoulders, neck, jaw and tongue all affect alignment. Alignment affects breath, which finally affects the vocal folds. The overworked folds eventually experience inflammation, swelling, fatigue and finally loss of sound. That thick or scratchy feeling you feel at the end of a long rehearsal is vocal fatigue generally caused by the body working too hard to overcome the effects of tension.

Where does the tension come from? Just the fact that we, as human beings, walk upright in defiance of gravity creates tension as we move through the day. Each vertebra is pulled toward the earth, causing the spine to compress. The weight of the head, twelve to fourteen pounds (about the size of a Christmas goose), is pulled forward. The shoulders move closer to the earlobes, the back of the head sinks on to the top of the spine, the intercostal muscles that separate the ribs shorten, the chest falls toward the stomach, the knees lock and the ankles tighten. With this collapsing of space in the body comes a collapse of the voice as well. The voice has less space in which to live, less space to gather energy and vibrancy, less resonance, less volume and less brilliance. When space inside the body diminishes, the jaw, tongue and vocal folds jump in to compensate, to help push the voice. This compensation only creates more tension, tightness and effort. The voice gets thin or strident, and it may feel scratchy and fatigued.

The simple activities of daily living – getting ourselves off to school or work each day, performing well in class, staying fit and pleasing teachers, bosses, parents and friends – all cause the body and the voice to tighten. It is impossible to live in this world tension-free. But it is possible to soften the body and the breath, to let the jaw hang loose, and to relax the tongue away from the hard palate. These simple, specific adjustments throughout a stress-filled day can make a huge difference. Releasing tension is a constant commitment and a daily challenge, and it is crucial to achieving a strong, clear voice.

Quickly and easily, the three best ways to release tension from the body and create space for the voice are to stretch, shake and breathe. In the following exercises, we will do a little of each. As you work, focus each exhale on a gentle f-f-f sound at your lips, and the inhale will take care of itself.

⊙ Relaxation exercise 1: *Basic relaxation exercise* (DVD)

Teacher tip
Always start voice work with some variation of this basic exercise. It brings the students to presence and shakes away enough tension and distraction to begin the work.

- Shake your hands.

- Shake one foot, then the other.

- Move your hips in a big circle.

- Roll your shoulders.

- Stretch up on your toes, arms reaching toward the sky.

- Reach out into the space as if carving through the air.

- Sigh out a huge sound of relief.

Relaxation exercise 2: *Internal space awareness*

> **Teacher tip**
> *Work through this exercise slowly, encouraging students to be thoroughly present. You may want to play music that sets the tone, such as "In Paradisum" by Fauré, the "Miserere" by Allegri or "Fantasia on a Theme of Thomas Tallis" by Vaughan Williams.*

In order for the voice to work in its most efficient and effective way, a feeling of space must be continually created in the body: space in the mouth, space in the neck, space up the spine, space between the ribs, space between the shoulders and earlobes, space across the shoulder girdle, space in the joints, space in the torso, space in the lungs, and space in the abdomen. These are naturally occurring spaces in the body that collapse and get smaller as we pick up tension through the course of the day. Drawing awareness to inner space begins to free the voice as it relaxes the body. A quick note about volume and filling a large space: the more inner space you carry with you, the more power you will have to fill the larger space outside you.

As you work through this exercise, remember to breathe – imagine that you can breathe into the spaces you are creating. Close your eyes so you can better envision the inside of the body.

○ Stand with feet shoulder-width apart, knees released, eyes closed.

○ Think of the top of the head floating up as if filled with helium, the face forward, the back of the neck long. Imagine that your neck is growing skyward with chin parallel to the floor.

○ Feel the jaw relaxed and hanging loosely from the skull. Allow the tongue to rest on the floor of the mouth with the tip behind and gently touching the bottom teeth.

○ Feel the weight of the shoulders giving in to gravity; be aware of the distance between your shoulders and earlobes.

○ Imagine a ball of energy moving out from the middle of the shoulders, widening and lengthening the shoulder girdle.

○ Imagine that your upper arm is moving away from your shoulders, the lower arm moving from your elbow, your hands moving away from your wrist.

○ See your ribcage as a large airy barrel surrounding your spine; imagine your lungs as two large balloons filled with air.

○ Imagine that your spine is growing in two directions as the head floats to the sky, the tailbone toward the earth. Be aware of the space between the vertebrae.

- Be aware of the space between your hips and your torso. Imagine that the torso can move up and away from the hips.

- Feel the space between your thighs and shins.

- Imagine that the feet are spreading out against the floor.

- Relish how tall and light you feel as you find space inside the body; breathe into all the new-found spaces.

- With this new sense of inner space, let a breath drop in and speak: count one to ten, say your whole name, or speak a line of two of a monologue. Be aware of changes in your sound.

Throughout this work, I will remind you of the importance of creating space within the body that matches the size of the space you wish to fill with sound. This sensation is one you want to maintain as you do this vocal work. Even when performing, if you start to feel that the voice is not working just right, simply "think space" and you allow the voice to move to a more efficient place.

Discussion questions

What in your body feels different now than it did before? How would you describe how you feel right now? Was there a part of the exercise where you sensed a feeling of inner space? What has changed in your voice?

Relaxation exercise 3: *Isolation of body parts*

- Stand with your feet parallel, hip-width apart, with your weight evenly distributed over both feet.

- Let a breath drop into your body and let out a robust sigh of relief; this brings your mind and breath into the body. Sigh out several more times, on voice: a hearty "ahh". With each sigh, feel a deeper sense of relief.

The neck, where the vocal folds are housed, is a huge repository of tension. The goal here is to maximize your sense of space in the back of the head and neck. Each of the release exercises below should be repeated with gentle to moderate effort at least ten times.

- Let your chin drop to your chest and shake your head, "no". Be aware of the gentle pull between the shoulders.

○ Let your ear float near your shoulder, then drop your chin back to the chest and let your other ear float to the other shoulder, as if you are inscribing a "happy face" in the air with the top of your head. It is rather like a "suspend and fall" movement: the movement of the head suspends over one shoulder, and then falls as the chin returns heavily to the chest.

○ Inscribe a circle in the air with the tip of the nose. Start with a small circle, then let it get larger.

○ Bosco Bob: Imagine the funny little toy dog that you often see in the back of car windows, its little head bobbing easily from right to left. (I call this the Bosco Bob in honor of my cocker spaniel Bosco who always has lessons to teach me about release and relaxation.)

○ Head float: Feel the top of the head floating up as if filled with helium; the sensation of "long back of neck, soft front of neck" is key and recurrent in the work. The face is forward, eyes on the horizon, as the back of the neck lengthens toward the sky. Be aware of space between the head and shoulders and the space between the vertebrae in the neck.

The shoulders are a favorite spot for tension collection. As I go through the day, I find my shoulders getting closer and closer to my earlobes. As I sit at the computer, listen to an animated student or a frustrated colleague, or answer an advising question, I can feel that space getting smaller and smaller. Follow the steps below to enhance the space above and below the shoulders. Again, ten repetitions is our magic number.

○ Circle the shoulders slowly, putting all your concentration into a controlled perfect circle. Feel the shoulder joint getting looser and wider as the size of your circle increases. Feel as though you can lubricate the shoulders with breath. Reverse the circle.

○ Bounce the shoulders gently, lifting them high to the earlobes and dropping them low and heavy.

○ Swing one arm in a large circle like a windmill, first in one direction, then the other. Swing the other arm.

○ Shake your hands by relaxing at the wrist and gently flapping up and down.

○ Tighten your hands to make claws, then clench your fists, and shake them out. I call this, in fond memory of a beloved teacher, Irene Comer, "Claw, Clench, and Throw Away'".

Torso and spine A physical therapist once told me that you are only as healthy as your spine. Keeping the spine supple and flexible with these simple daily exercises is part of that process for the good of the voice and the good of your general health. The following sequence should be worked through with an awareness of creating space between ribs, space between vertebrae, and a general openness and expansion of the torso.

○ With arms loosely out from the body, gently twist from side to side, increasing flexibility in the spine. This is a relaxed movement; do not throw your body from side to side, just let it go there.

○ Snake the spine: Roll down the spine slowly, feeling the head giving in to gravity, one vertebra at a time, knees bent, head and arms remaining free all the way down. Shake out some sound, feeling it fall from the top of your head. Sigh out a deep sigh of relief. Roll up slowly from the base of the spine, again focusing on length and space. The neck and head are the last to come up. Be aware of the easy natural alignment of the spine, neck and head as you come to standing.

○ Ribs: To open the intercostal muscles (the muscles that connect the ribs), reach your right arm over your head and stretch it toward the left. Keep your knees relaxed as you imagine breathing into your exposed ribcage. Hold the stretch for five breaths. Imagine that you are "presenting the ribcage", as if showing that exposed ribcage to the world. Then vigorously pat the ribcage. Let your arms relax at your side. Allow a deep breath to drop into your torso. Does the stretched side move more in response to the breath?

○ Repeat the stretch-and-pat on the other side. When both arms return to your side, be aware of the sense of lift and expansion in the ribs. You have created more space for the lungs to inflate with air.

○ To release the hips and pelvic girdle and create a sense of inner space, move your hips in a big, sloppy circle, ten times in one direction and ten in the other. The knees stay released. Add an easy hum with your lips together, teeth apart. Open the sound to an "aah", letting the sound mirror the circle of the hips.

○ Pelvic rock and roll: Using the image of a porch swing, move the pelvic girdle forward and back. Exhale as the pelvis swings forward, inhale as the pelvis swings back. Twenty repetitions. You can also add an "aah" or "ooh" as you easily let the pelvis rock forward and back.

○ Swing the hips from side to side. Add an easy sound like "whee" as you freely swing the hips.

○ Put a gentle shake in your hips to give a final loosening to the whole area. Add an easy "ahh" as you move.

○ Lift your foot and circle at the ankle, first in one direction, then in the other. Think of a perfect circle in your ankle. Imagine that you can draw breath up through the sole of your foot. Repeat ten times in each direction with each ankle. Enjoy the space you have created between the foot and the rest of the leg. You can also add a hum as you circle the foot.

○ Swing your leg back and forth – don't dance or try to make it a lovely movement, just enjoy moving your leg back and forth. Think of lubricating the hip socket with breath; imagine that the space in the hip is growing larger with each swing. Shift your weight to the other foot, and repeat the swing. Shake each leg vigorously as if kicking off a flip-flop. Add an easy "ahh" as if shaking sound out your foot.

With the above exercises, you have loosened the body, released some of the tension that blocks the voice, gently warmed up your voice, and created inner space which will allow the voice to be more open, vibrant, resonant and clear.

Casper the friendly ghost

Let a tremor begin in your feet; let it travel up your leg to your knees. Feel the tremor travel first to your thighs, then to your hips. It moves to your belly and back, up to the shoulders and down your arms and hands. Finally it moves out from the top of your head. Add a ghost-like "ooh" that tremors freely as if a friendly ghost is announcing his presence. Repeat several times with softness and ease. A wave of easy energy and sound moves through the body.

Starfish

Releasing and stretching on the floor is a great way to start a voice class. Use mats if you have them. This is a guided imagery exercise using the extended metaphor of the starfish soaking up the warm rays of the sun and moving its six starfish appendages as it stretches in the warm, moist sand. I like to use easy classical music here to enhance the image and ease release, perhaps Beethoven's "Moonlight Sonata". (Allow fifteen minutes to explore this exercise fully.)

○ Lie on your back in a large "X" position, with your arms and legs spreadeagled. Focus on your breath. Release your weight into the warm, moist sand. Feel the sun warming your center. Feel the breath deep in your center as it responds to the golden rays of the sun. Feel your six starfish appendages stretch – those would be your two arms, your two legs, your head, and your tailbone. Imagine that the head and tailbone can reach the length of your arms and legs. Imagine yourself as a perfectly formed, six-point starfish lazing away the hours on the warm, moist beach.

○ One of your starfish limbs begins to move easily in the sand, reaching out, or even flicking sand in the air. This limb wants to explore the possibility of movement, stretching, reaching, and gently extending up, out and around. When it has explored the full range of starfish movement, it slowly settles back to the warm sand.

○ Then, in succession, each starfish limb, including the head and tailbone, explores easy range of motion – stretching up, out and over – before coming to rest.

- Perhaps then two limbs or all limbs move together in the easy way that a starfish might move across the sandy beach.

- Allow the starfish to come to rest, again feeling the golden rays of the sun warming your center.

- Roll to your side. Cradle your head in your arm. Breathe deeply before you prepare to roll up the spine to a sitting position.

- Roll up the spine to a standing position, find your feet and feel length in the spine. Speak a couple of lines of a monologue or simply count.

Kristina's blog

The idea of inner space was new to me. I have always been aware of filling the space outside me, especially when I sing. But I discovered that thinking bigger inside makes my voice bigger with a lot less effort. Starfish is one of my favorite exercises so far. I felt relaxed yet ready. I have always thought that I had to have tension in order to perform, but I was relaxed, and my voice was so strong.

Discussion questions

What did you notice as we proceeded through this exercise? What changes have happened? Do you feel differently? Did something change in the breath from the beginning to the end? Was there a change in the voice?

Teacher tip
This is a deeply relaxing exercise when given the time and the proper tone. You will want to follow it with an exercise that energizes, such as "Casper the friendly ghost" or circling the hips with a sound. The following exercise is also a good group-energizer.

Dialogue in sound and motion

This exercise releases body and voice and is a great energizer. Students work in pairs.

- Partner A performs a sound and a movement and tosses it to partner B.

○ B takes the sound and movement and transforms it into another sound and movement that she sends back to A.

○ The partners carry on a sound-and-movement conversation, using the whole body and an open, released sound.

Teacher tip

Encourage students to use full-body, abstract movement – it should not be literal or look like sign language. Sounds can be vowels, consonants or a mixture of both. If they begin to use constricted or throaty sounds that could be harmful, coach them to use open, free sounds. There is a balance between full-body and voice commitment while staying safe and healthy that you can help them find through side-coaching and modeling. It is an ongoing challenge for all acting, movement and voice teachers.

⊙ Seaweed (DVD)

The seaweed exercise releases physical and vocal tension and has the feeling of an imaginative game. For this sequence you will want to use music that inspires floating or swimming. This is a group activity that starts with each individual working separately; it becomes a partner exercise as it progresses. A narrative sets up the circumstances and side-coaching proceeds throughout. Allow fifteen minutes for this exercise. You will need to have a short memorized monologue or sonnet at the ready.

Teacher tip

Though this exercise is introduced as a relaxation exercise, I use it throughout as a resonance exercise, as an expressivity activity to shake up work that has gone stale, or simply for freeing the voice. The narrative is written below as a monologue that you might be reading to your class as you take them through this exercise. You may want to view the DVD to see how the narrative is used to help this exercise develop.

○ Space yourselves through the room so that each of you has the same amount of space.

○ Feel your feet against the floor as you close your eyes and tune into the breath. Take in the images but don't begin moving until instructed to do so.

○ Imagine that you are seaweed under the surface of the ocean. You are firmly rooted to the ocean floor but your seaweed body is free to float in the water. You can be easily buffeted by the changing currents. Your arms can float on the gentle support of the water. Your face, head and neck are supported by the water. Your back is weightless, your knees are loose. Go ahead and allow the gentle currents of the water to move you easily. Perhaps an arm floats toward the surface. Perhaps both arms. Your head bobs easily as it is supported by the gentle currents; your jaw releases; your tongue even feels that it can float. Your body can easily sway forward and back, your knees are soft, but your feet hold you solidly to the ocean floor.

○ A colorful school of small fish swims around you, whipping up the current and moving your seaweed body. The fish pass and the water settles, allowing you to return to your easy, floating life.

○ A large fish makes circles around you, churning up the water around your seaweed body. Your arms quickly rise toward the surface, your knees bend, and your head and neck circle while maintaining the ease of weightless floating.

○ If seaweed had a voice, what would it sound like? Try adding an open "ah" to accompany your seaweed movements. Are there other open vowel sounds that float out from the center of your seaweed body? If you are floating up, let the sound go up. If you are settling on the bottom of the ocean floor, let the sound go down as well.

○ What if your seaweed knows a sonnet or monologue? Let the words float out as the current continues to buffet you in the water. The words are free to float up and down as easily as your seaweed body floats in the gentle currents.

○ Now open your eyes, feel your own natural alignment come back into your body. Connect with your breath and simply say the monologue, resisting any temptation to act. Just let it be whatever it wants to be.

⊙ Seaweed with a partner (DVD)

○ Find a partner. Partner A is the seaweed, partner B is the current. Partner A closes their eyes and gives the body over to the image of the seaweed floating under the water. Partner B gently touches a shoulder, elbow, wrist or knee. Partner A responds by allowing the body part touched to move easily as if affected by a change in the current. Repeat this several times.

○ Partner A adds open vowel sounds as partner B continues to provide the pulses of the current.

○ Partner A adds the words of their monologue or sonnet, as partner B continues to provide the pulses of the current.

○ Partner A: find your feet and come back into a sense of your own natural alignment. Open your eyes, face your partner and speak your monologue or sonnet, resisting any temptation to act. Just share the words with your partner.

○ Reverse so that B is the seaweed and A provides the pulse of the current. Repeat the instructions above.

Discussion questions

How does the body feel after this exercise? What changes happened in the voice? Where in the body does the voice feel most alive? What changes occurred in pitch range? What changes happened in the quality of the voice? What were the shifts or changes that revealed themselves as you spoke your monologue?

Colin's blog

I know I typically carry a lot of tension in my body. I had no idea that tension was holding back my voice. After we completed the release exercises my voice just felt easier, freer and clearer. I was surprised that I also felt more focused. My monologue was more natural too. I didn't sound so actor-ish. Go figure.

Reflective voice blog

What did you learn about your body and the release work? What was different in the way you felt physically, emotionally and mentally after the exercises? What questions came up for you as you worked? Did any comments from the rest of the class impact your learning today? Which exercises worked best for you?

Chapter 4 references

For more information on the topics discussed in this chapter refer to:

Boston, Jane, and Cook, Rena, eds, *Breath in Action: The Art of Breath in Vocal and Holistic Practice*. London: Jessica Kinsley Publishers, 2009.

Carey, David, and Clark Carey, Rebecca, *Vocal Arts Workbook and DVD*. London: Methuen Drama, 2008.

Gronbeck-Tedesco, John, *Acting Through Exercises*. Mountain View: Mayfield Publishing Company, 1992.

Linklater, Kristin, *Freeing the Natural Voice*. Hollywood: Drama Publishers, 2006.

McAvenue, Kelly, *The Actor and the Alexander Technique*. New York: Palgrave Macmillan, 2002.

Rodenburg, Patsy, *The Actor Speaks*. London: Methuen Drama, 1997.

Exercises

"Starfish" and "Seaweed" are based on work taught by Debbie Green and Morwenna Rowe at the Central School of Speech and Drama, London.

5 But that's how I always stand!

Our bodies speak volumes about us. The shape of the spine (whether it is long and straight or hunched and rounded), the position of the shoulders and the lift of the chin shout to the world about our level of confidence, social effectiveness, health and emotional maturity. Other people may even make assumptions about personal discipline and intelligence based on how we carry ourselves. I am speaking here of alignment, or what your parents and teachers might refer to as posture.

The basic concept is that our body parts – head, neck, shoulders, ribcage, hips, knees and feet – are naturally organized in such a way as to counter the effects of gravity, to ensure ease of movement and maximum efficiency of breath. This also involves how the body's weight is carried, whether standing, sitting or moving through space. In voice terms, efficient alignment creates a foundation or platform upon which our body space is built. Lifting the body into its natural organizational relationship creates space for the diaphragm to move, space for breath in the lungs and space for resonance in the throat and mouth.

Many of us, if we are not aware of the power of alignment, allow our posture to deviate from the point of maximum efficiency. Our "familiar" alignment – that is, what we have grown accustomed to through years of habitual use – may be thwarting our vocal potential. The head may jut forward, the shoulders round or press back, the ribcage caves in or thrusts out, or the hips push to one side. The feet may not be making solid contact with the floor. You probably recognize yourself in one or more of these images and want to answer, "But Rena, this is just how I always stand; that's how I move naturally." It may be how you have grown accustomed to standing or moving, but it is not the most efficient way for your body to function. If you want maximum vocal effectiveness, you need to look at your alignment.

How we got this way

Throughout our lives, from our first steps onward, we have been forming habits of how we organize our bodies: how we stand, how we sit and how we move. We are responding to feedback we receive from parents and peers. We are fulfilling our social and psychological needs. We are defending ourselves against the natural stresses of existence. In short, we are trying to survive. In the midst of all this, we develop habits of alignment that may not serve us as we work toward maximizing the voice.

In contrast to your familiar alignment, I want to discuss "natural" alignment. Notice I don't use the term "proper alignment", because we are not talking about something that is rigid and stiff, with shoulders thrown back and chest held high. It is not based on that childhood memory of a parent or teacher admonishing us to "stand up straight". Natural alignment comes from the feeling that the body is moving up as it moves forward. The top of the head floats and lifts toward the sky as if helium balloons are tied to the base of the skull. The head sits easily on top of the spine, the face is forward, eyes alert meeting the world, the shoulders are relaxed and down, arms hang easily at the side, the pelvis is centered, neither tucked under or pushed back, the knees are released, and the feet are parallel, hip-width apart with weight evenly distributed.

Wow, for most of you what I have described probably seems foreign, weird, stuffy and pretentious. In truth however, it is not only the voice that is linked to natural alignment, but physical and mental health as well. If your familiar stance is caved, slouched or rounded, your digestion can't work as efficiently; your back is compromised, and this will eventually lead to stiffness and pain, if it isn't already giving you problems. Interestingly enough, our physical state informs our emotional state. If we meet the world in the body I described above, we will likely feel a lack of self-confidence, with dark, heavy or sad mood. We might even feel what I call "free-floating anxiety", when there is no reason to feel uneasy or irritable but we just do. Perhaps our alignment is affecting our ability to take a deep breath and we feel uneasy due to lack of oxygen.

An adjustment in our alignment can lead to an adjustment in our sense of well-being. When our lungs are given space to fully inflate, and breath moves freely and deeply, it clears the anxiety chemicals from the body. And of course, with a healthy breath comes a healthy voice.

Exercise for alignment

The following pages take you through natural alignment in detail. While working through these exercises, maintain a sense of ease as you go from your familiar alignment to your natural alignment.

Feet

- Start with a grounded base, maintaining awareness of the feet in solid contact with the earth. Imagine that energy is drawn up through the soles of the feet; the whole of the earth is supporting the body as it speaks and moves.

- Place the feet parallel, hip-width apart.

- Shift your weight back and forth from one foot to the other several times. Rock forward and back from toes to heels. Find that place where the weight is evenly balanced over both feet. Imagine the bones in the foot spreading out across the floor.

45

o Imagine that the base of the big toe, the base of the little toe, and the heel form a solid triangle of support. Keeping the knees released, stand firmly on that base and relish the sense of strength it gives you.

Knees

o Release your knees with a gentle bounce – I call it "finding oingo-boingo" in your ankles and knees. Be aware of space and "cush" (a spongy feeling) in the joints.

o Just for jollies, lock your knees and try to breathe. With your knees still locked say, "Good morning, I am so pleased to be here today." Now release the knees, take a breath and say, "Good morning, I am so pleased to be here today." It should be clear that the locked knees make deep breathing more difficult, and that vocal ease, volume and clarity are adversely affected.

It is natural to lock the knees under the pressure of performance: it is part of the "fight or flight" mechanism that kicks in. A trained voice user knows to "release, release, release" at the start of (and at key points during) the presentation or performance.

Release of the knees should not be confused with bent knees. A speaker does not have to go through life with permanently bent knees. It is a simple release as opposed to a lock. Go back and forth between locked and released to become more aware of the difference.

Pelvic girdle and tailbone awareness

As we continue our quest for natural, efficient alignment, finding the freest place for the pelvic girdle to live becomes a bit of a challenge. We are not as aware of this area of the body as we are of our head, neck and shoulders. This part of the body is not spoken of as we grow up, not included in our parents' awareness of us as we are learning to walk, and is generally avoided and ignored. It houses the sex organs and consequently carries with it an acculturated tension to hide and deny the energy that lives in the area. In the use of the free and released voice, it provides the floor of the inner space that we are attempting to create. The pelvic girdle contains a key to release and a key to support – both crucial components in the development of the voice.

Common problems in this area have to do with the holding of muscles and habitual pelvic tilts, either too far forward or too far back. Each of these leads to breath problems and blockage of the potential vocal resonance that make the voice fuller, richer and louder. Ideally, a speaker wants to sound as if the whole torso – all the way to the pelvic floor – is involved in creating the voice.

The following exercises will increase your sensory or kinesthetic awareness of the pelvic girdle and the tailbone. They will also help you find length in the lower spine and feel where the most efficient and released position exists for you.

○ Focus your imagination on the tailbone, the end of the spine. Imagine that it has the ability to look behind you, in front of you, or at the floor.

○ Extend the pelvic girdle forward so the tailbone eye can see the wall in front of you. Push the pelvic girdle back so the eye of the tailbone can see the wall behind you. Then allow the tailbone to look at the floor. Repeat this several times till you get a sense of where the tailbone is. Finally you want to develop a comfort with allowing the tailbone to look at the floor beneath you. Feel the tailbone grow toward the floor. This is a gentle releasing sensation rather than a pressing.

○ Shake the tailbone to release any tension that may have been picked up in the above sequence as you can sound an "ahh".

○ Imagine the tailbone has a long string attached to it. At the end of the string is a lead ball bearing. Swing your hips so that the ball bearing moves in a small circle. Continue to swing the hips making larger and larger circles with the ball. Continue to swing the hips as the ball makes smaller and smaller circles. Allow the string and the ball to hang straight toward the floor. This is an efficient position for the tailbone and the pelvic girdle in order to provide the strongest, most open base for the voice. It is a position of grounding and power.

Spine

Another quick review of alignment so far: we have our feet firmly grounded to the floor, our knees released, and length in the lower spine as the tailbone reaches toward the floor. Turn your focus to the spine, which is the central core of the body, the central core of your vocal power and the central source of inner space.

○ Imagine the base of the spine: think your way up the spine, one vertebra at a time, think "lift", think "float", all the way to the top of the head. It is as if your spine is growing from the top and the bottom. The tailbone is moving toward the earth, the head is moving toward the sky. The face is still forward, eyes open to meet the world.

○ Take a walk round the room, feeling the power in the spine. Your face is leading you forward, and the top of the head is leading you up. Be aware of the space between the vertebrae. Imagine you are taller. The feet are in firm contact with the floor; your arms are moving easily at your side.

○ Stop and realign; think about the feet in solid contact with the floor, weight evenly distributed, knees released, length in the lower spine, the upper spine moving toward the sky, arms relaxed at your sides.

Shoulders

o Check to see that the shoulders are relaxed and down, the chest is wide and the arms are hanging at your side.

o Bounce the shoulders several times up and down. Feel the weight as they come up toward the earlobes; drop the weight heavily as they give in to gravity. Vocalize an "aah" as you jostle the shoulders up and down.

o Round the shoulders forward. Just for jollies, attempt to breathe and say your now-familiar line, "Good morning, I am so pleased to be here today."

o Push the shoulders back. Again, attempt to breathe and say your line. Hopefully, in either position breathing and making sound were not easy.

o Bounce the shoulders up and down again and relax them in the down position. Feel the width of the chest. Breathe and say your line, "Good morning, I am so pleased to be here today." You should feel that breath is easier and sound is fuller.

Head

My students often get tired of hearing "Long back of neck, soft front of neck." But this is the position that creates the most space in the throat and back of mouth. It is hard to maintain, particularly when we get animated and return to old vocal "press habits". Many of us are chin-leaders. We press, stress and emphasize with our chin. As soon as the chin comes up, we have closed off the space in the throat and the back of the mouth. The jaw becomes tense, as does the tongue. The voice gets brittle, shrill, tight or under-projected. From this position, the vocal folds have to do extra duty which can fatigue them, inflaming them or causing them to swell with the effort.

o As you explore the sensation of "long back of neck, soft front of neck", be aware that your jaw is released and the tongue is resting on the floor of the mouth.

o Gently look right and left several times. Look down and up several times. Find a place of balance as the head rests on the top vertebra. The head is balanced when it won't drop backward or forward.

o Drop the chin to the chest and shake your head "no". Slowly let it lift back to neutral.

o Let your right ear drop gently toward your right shoulder, and exhale on a "shh" sound. Let the head float back to neutral. Allow your left ear to drop gently toward the left shoulder, exhaling on a "shh" sound. Again, let the head float back to neutral. Do this slowly several times.

o Do the "Bosco Bob" we learned in the last chapter.

Putting it all together

Natural alignment is an ideal; it is a starting point. Actors often deviate from this as we get increasingly engaged in character transformations. But we start from and return to this place of natural alignment throughout a performance, knowing this is the place of maximum inner space, support, ease and efficiency. Let's run through it quickly:

- Feet are in solid contact with the floor.
- There is "oingo-boingo" in the ankles and the knees.
- There is length in the lower spine as the tailbone lengthens toward the floor and the spine extends upward, floating toward the sky.
- The shoulders are relaxed and down, arms hanging at your sides.
- The head floats on top of the spine with long back of neck and soft front of neck.
- The jaw is relaxed, and the tongue is resting on the floor of the mouth.
- The breath is flowing easily.
- Take a walk through the room and enjoy the sensation of ease, energy, lightness.
- Stop and realign. Try a bit of a monologue or poem, or count easily one to ten.
- Walk again briskly – not zombie-like, but alert and ready to do a job.
- Stop and try the monologue or poem again.
- For contrast's sake, try walking in your "familiar" alignment, your habitual walk, and say the same bit of speech as you walk.
- Now recover your "natural alignment", again creating space in the spine. Aware that breath is flowing in your body, walk briskly and say the speech. Go back and forth several times between familiar and natural alignment. Be aware of the differences in the effort, quality and volume of your sound.

⊙ Grounding and aligning with dowel rods (DVD)

Before I take you through this exercise, I want to tell you that at first you are going to hate me; when we are done you are going to love me. I have had students proclaim that they never understood natural alignment until we did this!

For this exercise you will need a dowel rod half an inch in diameter, two to three feet in length (these can readily be found at hardware or home-improvement stores).

Before we start, let's do a little pre-test, a check-in to get a baseline reading of what the body feels like at this very moment. We will do this exercise with our shoes off.

49

○ Close your eyes and be aware of your feet against the floor. Be aware of your knees: are they locked or soft? No need to change anything at this point – just be aware. Send your attention to your hips and lower back. Is there tension or pain or stiffness?

○ With your eyes still closed, picture your spine as if you are drawing it from the base of the spine to the vertebrae in your neck. Imagine your head as it balances on top of the spine. Be aware of your jaw and tongue.

○ Send your attention to your breath. Is it deep or shallow? Where are you most aware of breath entering and leaving your body? Don't change anything yet, but be aware.

○ Be aware of any emotions you might be feeling. Fatigue, boredom, anxiety, excitement?

○ Open your eyes. Allow your toes to hang over the rod, breathing deeply, softening the jaw and tongue, and thinking about a long easy spine. Slowly walk across the dowel rod, lingering for a count of fifteen at toes, ball of the foot, two places in the arch, and the heel, surrendering to any discomfort until feet are flat on the floor once more. For variety you can exhale on a "shh" or "v", breath out a sigh of relief as you move to the next point on the foot, or even vocalize on an easy "ha ha ma ha ha". These are distractions from the discomfort of the exercise and provide an opportunity to begin the warm-up of the voice easily.

Teacher tip

I have found that this is one of the most powerful and telling of the alignment exercises. At first it meets with resistance because walking across the dowel rod is not comfortable and the more tension we have in our feet the more discomfort we are likely to feel. I now do a whole series of easy vocal warm-ups as we walk across the rod, focusing first on head-rolls, then shoulder-rolls, then a few simple breathing exercises, finally into easy sounding. It is important to take time to discuss the "before and after" of this exercise to reinforce how sensations and awareness have shifted in the body. This exercise is featured on the DVD.

○ When you step off, be aware of what is different in the feet, the knees, the hips, lower back, top of head, jaw, shoulders, breath. Do the feet feel different against the floor? What is your sense of how your alignment is now organized? Is the breath flowing more freely? Have your emotions shifted any? Some students report that anxiety lifts a little and that focus is clearer; they feel more present.

The first time I did this exercise as a student, I cursed the teacher under my breath the whole time. But when I stepped off the rod and felt my feet in contact with the floor, I was amazed. I finally knew what it felt like to be truly grounded! The release of tension went up through my entire body. I later learned that all the nerve endings in the body find their way to the feet. Walking across the dowel rod is like a massage; the entire body benefits. Natural alignment happens . . . well, naturally.

Colin's blog

Today we were introduced to the dowel rod! A very inter-esting tool that I had never used before and was quite excited to explore. We walked out the tension in our feet by standing on the rod first with the balls of the feet, then our arches and then our heels. This was a great oppor-tunity to see how the rod affected both our stance and our breathing. I was never more aware of my feet! Every part was in contact with the floor. Believe it or not, an hour before my audition I took out my broom in my apartment and used this exercise so I would feel completely free of tension.

Kristina's blog

When we pulled out the dowel rod and stood on it with different parts of the feet, not only did the class feel an immediate reaction to it, but I was completely amazed. I have never felt so free of tension in my feet and lower body before. I am a huge runner and I am often a little sore in my legs and back. Also, I had been a little happy/anxious/nervous/stressed about the start of school, so I had some tension in my upper body. I also clench my jaw when I am mad or nervous. Then we walked across the dowel rod. OH MY GOSH! I have never felt so much tension go away so quickly, especially in my legs and shoulders!

Reflective voice blog

Record what you experienced as you worked through the alignment exercises. What are your thoughts about your familiar alignment vs your natural alignment? At what point did you feel the most change or shift? Where in the body are you most aware of change? What is happening with the breath? Have your feelings or emotions shifted at all?

Grounding and centering

Many voice and acting teachers, even directors, will refer to "grounding and centering". "That actor is not grounded." "She has not found her center." "If you can just stay grounded, your acting will be fine." "Don't go off your center; you are losing your power." If you were to ask these speakers what they meant by those terms, they would all have slightly different answers.

Being "grounded", as I define it, is a solid connection with the floor. The actor knows where her feet are and she is drawing power from that connection. Imagine for a moment that your feet are not only standing squarely on the floor, with feet hip-width apart, weight evenly distributed over both feet, but that you are also standing on a mirror image of yourself, feet resting on and being supported by the feet of your other self. Feel the full weight of your other self supporting you. Breathe deep in your belly and sense that powerful connection. This is grounded. Need another image? The sensation you felt after you walked across the dowel rod – that is grounded!

Centering has to do with awareness and engagement of the middle portion of your body – your center of gravity if you will – which for most of us is in the abdominal area, slightly below the navel. It is the center and source of your strength and power. When you are centered, this part of the body is alert, energized. By breathing deeply into your center, you can find the state of relaxed readiness that I mentioned earlier. You are ready to spring into action, to respond to any stimulus, move in any direction, and speak any line with authentic power. All movement is initiated from your center, and all authentic and stage-worthy emotions come from your center. To get a quick sense of this, go to the wall.

- Place both hands on the wall just below shoulder height, as if you were going to do a push-up off the wall.

- The spine is straight, the neck released, and shoulders down. Now think in terms of an effort level of about three (on a scale of one to ten, ten being the most effort you are capable of, one being the least), breathe into your lower belly and press into the wall as you exhale. Feel the energy coming from your center and traveling out through your hands. Do this several times.

- Then, as you press against the wall, count out loud from one to five. Feel the power of your sound coming from your center. Imagine that you have an open and released tube from your center out through your mouth. Imagine the sound penetrating the wall. Be sure that your shoulders stay down and your effort level remains in the range of three to five. Do this several times and feel the connection between your center and the power of your sound.

○ Find a partner of fairly equal height and weight. Face your partner at a distance of the reach of both your arms. Put your hands together, and press, at the same number-three effort level. The goal is not to do combat or push your partner off balance. Be aware of the effort in your center.

○ Keep your shoulders down, hands slightly below shoulder height, and your back straight. Breathe into your center, count out loud from one to five. Alternate several times with your partner. Feel the relationship between your effort and the energy you feel in the center. That energy is the muscle engagement of "centering". Be aware of the power and ease of your sound.

⊙ Grounding with drums (DVD)

This exercise is done to the slow, steady, rhythmic beat of drums. I use track ten of a CD called "Chakra Breathing Meditations" by Layne Redmond. It involves a sequence of six lunges coupled with an open "hah" vocalization.

○ Start from a grounded position – feet firmly planted, spine long, shoulders relaxed – with the arms out, rounded, full of energy as if hugging a large tree.

○ To the rhythm of the recorded drum beat, lunge right, extend your right arm, and allow a rich, open "hah" to be vocalized from your center as the right foot lands. Come back to center.

○ Lunge left, extend your left arm, and allow the same rich, open "hah" to sound as the left foot lands on the floor, then come back to center. This sequence continues with a lunge forward on a right diagonal, then forward on a left diagonal, then back on the right diagonal, and finally back on the left diagonal. Each lunge is followed by a return to center. The entire sequence starts again. Throughout the exercise the eyes follow the moving hand. Continue for two to three minutes

Be aware of what you feel when you stop this exercise. How would you describe it? Where do you feel more energized? Are there parts of the body that feel more open? What happened to the voice as this exercise progressed?

Colin's blog

The drum exercise really helped me free up my center and be able to breathe freely and with even more focus. It was as if every time I breathed it became easier. The whole center of my body felt huge!

Forward inclination and natural alignment (DVD)

A simple and quick way to find natural alignment is through a forward inclination, which some teachers call the spinal zipper.

○ Stand with your feet hip-width apart, weight evenly distributed, long spine, released neck. Breathe slowly and deeply throughout this exercise.

○ Let your chin drop to your chest. Slowly giving in to gravity, let the spine incline forward one vertebra at a time until the head and neck are dangling free. The arms are released, the knees are bent, and you are breathing deeply. Sigh out as if the sound could just fall from the mouth.

○ Start to rebuild the spine from your tailbone, stacking one vertebra on top of the other like building blocks; the head is the last to come up. When the spine and shoulders are fully erect, lift the head, feeling long back of neck, soft front of neck, and a released jaw. Breathe into your center.

How does this feel? What does this do for your sense of alignment? Does the spine feel longer? What is happening with the lower spine? The pelvic girdle? The jaw?

Find natural alignment on the floor

Another interesting way to bring your body into natural alignment is to lie down on the floor. Although you can do this alone, I will describe the work for partners. If you are working through this in a class, find a partner. One of you will lie down on the floor, carpet or mat. The other will be assisting.

Teacher tip

Hands-on partnering is an important part of the vocal development process. Partners help us to be more aware, call our attention to things we have forgotten, or help us release tension spots which we may not be aware of. That being said, I know that it can be tricky to ask students to touch one another. Those of you who teach know exactly what I am talking about. I set the stage for this type of work before I begin by acknowledging that mature and focused behavior is required to maximize the benefit we may get from an exercise. I let them understand that students of all ages who engage in voice training can do these types of exercises with a minimum of laughter and discomfort. I ask them to think like a professional performer and stay focused on doing the best they can for their partner. Then I explain that the following exercise will require that they assist their partner with gentle non-threatening touch. Of course, if there is a student who is clearly not comfortable with touching or being touched, they can simply observe the exercise without penalty or criticism. You know your group and need to follow your instincts on this issue.

- Partner A lies down on their back. Partner B sits near the head of Partner A.

- Partner A: feel the spine long against the floor, as if the head and the tailbone are gently growing away from each other. Feel the shoulders wide, arms relaxed easily at your sides, palms gently facing up. Let your feet roll out and let them easily flop open. Notice which parts of the body are touching the floor. Let your weight give in to the pull of gravity.

- Focus on the breath in the center of the body. Feel the belly rise as the breath comes in and the belly drop as the breath goes out.

- Partner B: slide your hands gently under the head of your partner as if to cradle it. Give an easy tug to lengthen the neck. Slowly turn your partner's head from side to side. Partner A: give up control of your neck and head to your partner. Let your jaw release, and continue to focus on the breath in your belly.

○ Partner B: move to your partner's right shoulder and slide both hands under the shoulder-blade. Gently jostle or bounce the shoulder, lifting it with both hands only an inch off the floor. Partner A: remain relaxed and focus on your breath. After fifteen seconds, gently lay the shoulder down. Press your hands gently on the top of the shoulder, encouraging it to release against the floor.

○ Partner B: move to the left shoulder of your partner and repeat.

○ Partner B: move to the feet of your partner, lift both ankles about four inches off the floor and gently jostle or bounce for about fifteen seconds. Gently lay the ankles down on the floor.

○ Partner A: be aware of the release of the body against the floor. Notice which parts of the body are touching the floor. Feel again a long spine and wide shoulders. What has changed? How has the breath changed?

○ As you prepare to stand, roll easily to your side, cradling your head in your arm. Take a couple of easy, deep breaths. Roll to your stomach for a couple of deep breaths. Slowly push yourself to all-fours. Settle back with your bum against your heels (in yoga terms this is the child's pose). Keeping your head down, roll up the spine to an easy standing position, with your feet parallel, hip-width apart, weight evenly distributed. Feel length in the lower spine, the middle and upper spine lengthening up, the head floating on top of the spine, the chin parallel to the floor, the eyes open, and the jaw relaxed. Breathe deeply into your center and sigh out on "haaa".

What has shifted in your sense of natural alignment? How is this different from your familiar alignment? Take a walk through the space. Feel tall and easy, long neck, face forward, eyes alert, breathing into your center. Stop and ground your feet, feeling your center alive and engaged.

Follow your partner

In this exercise, partners work together to help each other find natural alignment. When alignment is correct, there should be a straight plumbline from the earlobe to the top of the shoulder, through the top of the hip, to the middle outside edge of the foot.

○ Partner A assumes his/her natural alignment. Partner B observes to see if ear, top of shoulder, top of hip and middle of the foot fall

57

into a straight line, encouraging minor adjustments as necessary. Partner B encourages shoulder release by placing hands on top of shoulders and gently pressing down. If knees are locked, a gentle touch behind the knee can encourage release.

○ Partner B then shows Partner A what their alignment looks like by mirroring back what they see. They feed back to each other what they have noticed.

○ Partners switch and repeat the above sequence.

○ Partner A takes a walk around the space, using their familiar walk; B follows. They walk for several minutes, going in different directions, and varying the pace. If time and space allow, walk out of the room and down the hall. Partner B follows, paying close attention to Partner A's head and neck, shoulders, arms, spine and pelvis, legs and feet.

○ Partner B begins to take on the walk of A, imitating how A's alignment is carried into movement. This is not in an effort to make fun of A, but to witness and reflect back. B shows A how their alignment is carried into the walk. There is no note of judgment, just an exchange of information.

○ Partners switch and repeat the walk and observation.

A final word about natural alignment

Natural alignment may feel pretty different from your familiar. It may not be a change you want to make because "this is just the way I always stand". It is far easier to just continue doing what you've always done. However, natural alignment best serves the voice. It also best serves the wellness of the body and the mind. Our bodies were designed for maximum efficiency with minimal effort. All of our organs work better when we carry our bodies in natural organization. We breathe better, so we think clearer; we digest our food better, so we feel less sluggish. We take the stress and pressure off our backs, so we eliminate pain and stiffness. Natural alignment makes us look thinner (a particular favorite of mine). A little awareness as we go through our days – lengthening the neck, bringing the chin down, lowering our shoulders, releasing our knees – will go a long way to bringing us to a place where natural feels more like familiar.

Kristina's blog

The work on the mats really helped me grasp the concept of connection that the head, spine, tailbone and feet have. Only when we moved the tailbone correctly forward and backward were we able to impact the spine in the way we wanted. When we freed and relaxed the body, everything else fell into place. It is driving me crazy that I have a terrible habit of lifting my chin to speak. I mean, I am extremely happy that this class has made me aware of a bad vocal habit. Now I am working on fixing it. It still feels a little uncomfortable to lie "correctly". I notice that even when lying on the floor I experience a strong urge to tilt my chin up. I see now how much strain that puts on my voice, so I am going to fix it. I know it is going to just take practice.

Colin's blog

We worked on getting our natural alignment up and running. This consists of having the feet grounded to the floor, relaxing the shoulders, centering the pelvis and having a nice long back of neck. After each of us found our natural stance, we found a partner and observed their natural stance and helped them make any necessary adjustments. I noticed that my partner, like me, has a lot of tension in her shoulders. I tried to help her release some of that by giving them a good massage. The results were noticeable. The thing I most enjoyed was when our partners imitated our own alignment. It gave me a chance to see how I look from someone else's perspective. Very interesting!

Reflective voice blog

Now that you have worked through this series of exercises to help you experience natural alignment, write your thoughts, observations, questions, discoveries and frustrations in the space provided below. How did the group contribute to your learning? What are you going to take on board as part of your personal practice?

Chapter 5 references

For more information on the topics discussed in this chapter refer to:

Boston, Jane, and Cook, Rena, eds, *Breath in Action: The Art of Breath in Vocal and Holistic Practice*. London: Jessica Kinsley Publishers, 2009.

Bunch, Meribeth, *The Dynamics of the Singing Voice*, 4th edn. New York: SpringerWein, 1997.

Carey, David, and Clark Carey, Rebecca, *Vocal Arts Workbook and DVD*. London: Methuen Drama, 2008.

Linklater, Kristin, *Freeing the Natural Voice*. Hollywood: Drama Publishers, 2006.

McAvenue, Kelly, *The Actor and the Alexander Technique*. New York: Palgrave Macmillan, 2002.

Ocampo-Guzman, Antonio, "Alignment and the Actor", *Dramatics Magazine*, Educational Theatre Association, Vol. 78, No. 7 (March 2007).

Pierrot, April, "Effects of Posture on Diaphragmatic Breath", *Breath in Action: The Art of Breath, in Vocal and Holistic Practice*. London: Jessica Kinsley Publishers, 2009.

Rodenburg, Patsy, *The Actor Speaks*. London: Methuen Drama, 1997.

Exercises

The exercise "The Drums" was adapted from the work of Debbie Green and Morwenna Rowe, Central School of Speech and Drama, London.

6

If I weren't breathing, I'd be dead

Breathing is both the easiest and hardest task for an actor to master. When I first introduce the concept of breath for speech, no matter the age group, I get a response something like this: "But Rena, I already know how to breathe. If I weren't breathing I'd be dead." And I say: "Yes, but there are two types of breath: breath that sustains life, which you do involuntarily, and breath for speech, which we will learn takes a little more thought, practice and attention."

Sharing the voice on stage is a deep and personal thing; it takes courage, clarity of thought – and breath. So I am going to say this once and probably a million times more: "Breath is the single most important factor in the efficient use of the voice! If the breath is not working, nothing else will work." Breath is the cornerstone of the free and released voice, and no amount of talent, rehearsal time or sound systems can compensate for its absence. A responsive, flexible breath system translates directly to volume, quality, connection to authentic emotion and ease of delivery.

Even more than this, deep central breathing connects us to the center of who we are, to the core of the artist that lives inside each human being – in this case, the performing artist who shares thoughts, ideas, emotions, needs and actions. The physical action of the movement of the breath is a natural and automatic response to the need to share the voice. It is a beautifully complex, integrated system that through focus and daily practice can become as easy as . . . well, breathing.

How breath works

To help us understand how the breath works, let's imagine that the voice is like a trumpet. In order for the trumpet to sound you have to blow air into the mouthpiece. Breath is the power source. If you want the trumpet to be louder you blow more air. It is the same with the human voice – if you want a louder, fuller sound, you need more air.

There are essentially two kinds of breath that a person requires: passive breath for sustaining life, and active breath for speech. Breath to sustain life – both the inhale and the exhale – happens unconsciously with minimal effort; the body instinctively does its job of keeping us alive. Breath for speech differs in that both the inhale and the exhale are conscious and take a certain amount of energy and muscular engagement. It takes a great deal of energy and breath to speak lengthy ideas, communicate weighty emotions, or fill a huge theater with sound.

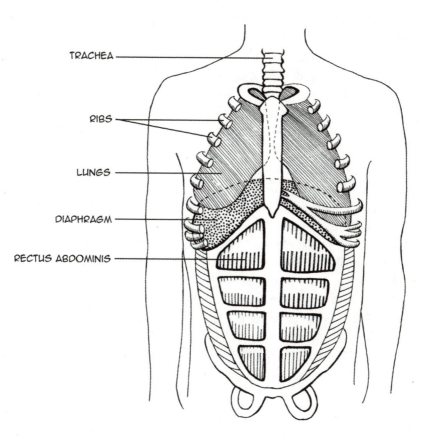

TRACHEA

RIBS

LUNGS

DIAPHRAGM

RECTUS ABDOMINIS

Key anatomical players of the breath system

The **diaphragm** is a large dome-shaped muscle that bisects the torso, positioned under the lungs and on top of the stomach.

The **intercostal muscles** link the ribs and allow them to move up and out to allow the lungs to fully inflate with air.

The **abdominal wall** includes the **rectus abdominis**, the **obliques**, and the **transverse** (a band of muscle just below the navel) – the muscles of breath support.

The **lungs** inflate with air on the inhale and deflate on the exhale. Our lungs have two lobes on the left and three lobes on the right. Ideally we need to fill all lobes, not just the top ones.

The **vocal folds** are the sound source, two flaps of tissue with a layer of muscle at the core that vibrate or oscillate when air blows past, creating tiny puffs of air, thus producing sound.

The **torso** extends from the shoulders to the pelvic girdle, to the ribs on either side, and to the breastbone in front and the spine in back. It houses the ribs, lungs, stomach and intestines.

Let's now review the anatomy of breath in a little more detail. When breathing for speech, the brain sends a signal that it would like to say something; it has a thought that needs to be communicated with the voice. The body then prepares to inhale in readiness for speech. A release of the **abdominal wall** follows, the **diaphragm** contracts and drops, and the **ribs** swing out and up. This action of the diaphragm and the ribs creates a negative pressure in the lungs. Air rushes into the lungs to equalize this pressure.

When the lungs have sufficient air, the process reverses and the exhale begins. It is on the exhale portion of the breathing cycle that sound occurs. The diaphragm relaxes and begins a passive journey back up to its resting place. The ribs move down and in. The muscles of the abdomen, primarily the **transverse**, engage to manage the exhale in terms of duration and the amount of air that leaves the lungs. This muscular action of the transverse is what we refer to as "support". When a choral conductor says, "Support your sound," or your drama director asks you to "use support", what they actually want is for you to engage the transverse to ensure you have adequate breath to support the voice for the length of the thought, sentence or phrase.

The air flow travels through the **windpipe**, where it meets the closed vocal folds. The air pressure, or what is called **subglottal pressure**, builds up, causing the vocal folds to blow open and snap closed hundreds of times per second, releasing tiny puffs of air, thus producing sound. Imagine that the words are carried out on a stream of breath. Breath and sound are one. When the exhale stops, the sound stops.

How breath goes wrong

Since we all breathe from the moment we are born, how can breath for speech go so wrong? Though there are many things that can derail an actor and her breath, I will discuss four major factors that thwart the free and released breath: 1) high, shallow breathing; 2) weak abdominal release; 3) lack of breath support; 4) generalized body tension.

When I was a young performer I noticed that when I auditioned my voice got thin and lost power. I also found myself having to take breaths in places I had not before. I now know that the culprit was **high, shallow breathing**. When we are nervous or experiencing stage fright many changes take place in the body. One of the first and strongest responses is the inability to take a deep breath. Under pressure, we instinctively resort to shallow breathing, which is counter-productive to good voice usage and also deepens our sense of performance anxiety. If your shoulders move up noticeably when you breathe in, you are filling only the top lobes of the lungs. That will not give you the breath capacity for a strong voice or the stamina to complete a complex thought without gasping for breath mid-sentence.

The majority of oxygen exchange happens deep in the bottom of the lungs. When we engage in high, shallow breathing, the oxygen never gets deep enough to nourish our brain, wake up our body, enliven our thoughts, trigger our creativity or calm our nerves.

I have also come to understand that high, shallow breathing prevents the performer from accessing the creative state – that place of honest connection to thought, impulses, action and emotions. Actors who have the ability to move an audience are connected to the creative state. In athletic terms, they are "in the zone". I can guarantee that a top performer in any field has mastered the art of breathing deeply.

Another way that breath for speech can go wrong is **weak abdominal release**, or not releasing the abdominal wall on the inhale. When the abdomen releases, the diaphragm has more space to make its trip down as it contracts, thus creating a larger space in the chest cavity for more air to enter the lungs. Many voice users initially do what I call reverse breathing: they suck the stomach in on the inhale and push it out on the exhale. This leads to shallow breathing and a reduction in the ability to support the sound. We will learn through the exercises below how an easy abdominal release on the inhale is our touchstone. Remember, as the breath comes in, the abdomen releases and goes out. On the exhale, the abdomen – specifically the transverse – engages and moves toward the spine.

Another way that breath for speech can go wrong is **lack of breath support** on the exhale, insufficient air moving past the vocal folds. We could call this poor breath management. When a strong, steady stream of air does not pass through the vocal folds, they have to work too hard, causing a distortion in the sound. The voice can then become pressed or strident, thin and small, or lacking in range of emotion, volume and quality. Lack of breath support can result in vocal fatigue at least and permanent damage to the vocal folds at the worst.

Finally I want to speak about how **generalized tension in the body** can sabotage the responsive breath. Locked knees, a rigid pelvic girdle, a tight stomach, a restricted ribcage and tension in the shoulders, jaw or tongue all inhibit the system. This kind of tension is insidious because we are often unaware of its presence; it is so common that it feels normal to us. Locking the knees is an unconscious response to standing for a long period of time; couple that with any level of performance anxiety, and those knees want to lock up tight. We have already mentioned that the shoulders tend to creep up to our ears because of the tension we pick up throughout the day. Tension anywhere in the body creeps into other parts, setting off a chain reaction until the whole body becomes a stress wad. Localized or generalized body tension prevents the abdominal muscles from fully releasing, keeping the diaphragm higher, creating less space for the lungs, which are then forced to take in smaller amounts of air, causing the vocal folds to do double duty. You get the picture.

The following exercises for the breath fall into seven categories:

1) connecting to the natural breath that sustains life

2) releasing the abdominal wall, which must precede the inhale

3) engaging rib release and rib swing

4) sensing the moment of readiness

5) engaging the transverse, which manages and supports the breath on the exhale

6) building breath capacity and sustainability

7) connecting breath to text

Connecting to the natural breath

⊙ The balanced breath – breathing through a straw (DVD)

The purpose of the exercise is to experience an easy, balanced breath while bringing attention to the natural movement of the abdominal area or – as we have called it – the center. You are going to inhale and exhale fully through a drinking straw.

- Gently hold the straw in the middle and put it between your lips.
- Exhale through the straw on a slow four count. Then inhale through the straw on a slow four count.
- As you inhale and exhale slowly through the straw, be aware of what is happening in your center: feel the movement. As you exhale, the center will move toward the spine. As you inhale, the center will release easily out.
- Repeat this for several minutes.

Teacher tip

Before I start this exercise, I address those students who may have panic issues associated with breathing. The idea that you are going to fully inhale and exhale through a straw can be anxiety-producing for some. I assure them that it is possible to fully breathe through the straw – I have never lost a student! I also warn that if they start to get dizzy they should reduce the effort; they may be working too hard. During the exercise I remind them to stay aware of what their centers are doing. They should be able to feel, in a natural way, that the abdomen expands on the inhale and contracts on the exhale. I generally don't do this exercise repeatedly, as I do some of the other breath exercises; its purpose is only to give a kinesthetic sensation of the natural movement of the center. During breath for speech the exhale is longer as we express ideas in language, and the inhale is very quick as the body prepares for the next thought. I also use this exercise to discuss the calming effect of deep, slow breathing. You may also want to point out that the temperature of the straw changes radically from inhale to exhale. The inhale is cooler, and the exhale is warmer, reflecting the profound warming effect that the body has on air that is often very cool.

Discussion questions

What did you notice about the movement of the center during this exercise? What happened to the breath? What shifts in the body have happened as a result of the exercise? State of mind or state of emotion – any changes there? The change in the temperature of the straw – what is that about?

Colin's blog

Rena handed us each a straw. We simply inhaled and exhaled through the straw, while being aware of what was going on in our centers. I loved this exercise! I felt that my breath capacity seemed to double as I did this. It was a huge eye-opener. It was also very relaxing. I asked why the temperature changed on the straw as we breathed – cold on the inhale and warm on the exhale. Rena said that the air is the temperature of the air around us as we breathe in. Then the body warms it to 98.6 degrees by the time we breathe it out. So the straw is cool as we breathe in and warm when we breathe out. Interesting.

⊙ Blow up the balloon (DVD)

The purpose of this exercise is to give you a strong sense of what the center does when you are breathing for speech.

○ Stretch the balloon so it will blow up more easily. Blow it up at your own pace, taking in a new breath when you need to. Be aware of what is happening in your center as you do this. When the balloon is full, quickly and easily empty the balloon.

○ Blow up the balloon again, this time putting your hand on your transverse muscle. Be aware of its movement and of how automatic it is. The abdomen expands as you inhale: the deeper the breath, the larger the expansion. On the exhale, the transverse engages and moves toward the spine.

Teacher tip

The balloon exercise, like the straw breath, I only use a couple of times. It is a quick way to reinforce kinesthetically how the abdominal muscles engage during breath for speech. Balloon work is fun, but you need to set some ground rules, as all students become children when they have balloons in their hands. Before I pass them out, I ask the students not to blow them up until I have given all the instructions. I also ask them not to inflate them so fully that they pop. When they are done, they squeeze it off until we have talked about what they experienced. After a brief discussion, I let them release the balloon in any way they want, giving them the opportunity to have the fun they have been waiting for.

Discussion questions

What happened in your center as you blew up the balloon? In which direction did you feel the center move on the exhale? Which direction on the inhale? What did you notice about abdominal release when you needed a new breath?

There are a couple of important points I want to discuss. First, when we are performing, we seldom need the amount of muscular engagement in the abdominals that you needed to blow up the balloon. Think of that as effort level ten. Even in shouting and speaking over crowd noise or music on stage you may only go to level eight. For normal stage speaking, you may only use effort level three or four. A truly responsive breathing system is easy and natural, happening without conscious thought on the part of the actor. That's why we train, to teach the body what it must do on its own – so that in the heat of performance, we are free to concentrate on the real issues of acting: what I want, how am I going to get it, and how my partner's response affects me.

Connecting to the natural breath, feeling abdominal release

Release of the abdominal wall is a challenging concept for a culture that worships the flat stomach. Many of us expend a lot of energy and effort to keep the stomach held in at all times. However, the actor must learn to cast that ideal aside and embrace a tummy that is relaxed, even (dare I say it) "poochie" on the inhale. On the inhale the stomach area expands; on the exhale the stomach moves toward the spine.

○ Stand easily in natural alignment and be aware of how you are breathing. Stay with this for at least ten breaths. Don't try to change it, just be aware of your own breath rhythm. Where are you most aware of the breath entering and leaving the body?

○ Place a hand just below your navel, and release the abdomen into your hand on each inhale.

○ Blow all the air out of your lungs on a "fff" or "shh", and wait until your body needs a breath. When your body signals that a breath is needed, release the abdominal wall and feel a breath drop in. Repeat this sequence ten times: blow out all the air, wait for the need to breathe, and then allow a breath to drop in. You should feel the abdomen release and expand on each new inhale.

○ Now let the natural breath rhythm just happen – the breath comes in, the breath goes out. Be aware of the pause that occurs after each cycle – breath comes in, breath goes out, pause. Repeat several times.

○ Continue exploring the breath cycle – the breath comes in, breath goes out, pause. Enjoy the pause, luxuriate in it, and wait gently for the need to start the cycle again. Notice that the quality of the pause determines the quality of the next inhale. Keep your knees soft, the back of the neck long and the jaw hanging loose. Breathing in this way should feel natural and easy.

Exploring the natural breath, connecting to abdominal release

Floor breath

○ Lie on the floor with legs and feet straight out. If you have lower back issues and it is more comfortable, you can place your feet flat on the floor and your knees up. Your face should be looking toward the ceiling. Close your eyes and be aware of your weight against the floor. Allow a heavy feeling to pull you into the floor, a peaceful and easy giving in to gravity.

○ Think long spine as you imagine that the head and tailbone are moving away from each other. Think space in the neck, and breathe deeply. Think about space between the shoulderblades; breathe deeply as if you could send breath into your shoulders.

Teacher tip

This is a very important exercise and you will want to go back to it frequently. Mats, if you have them, make the exercise more comfortable. Carpet is nice, but floor will work at a pinch. Establish a tone of easy relaxation. I try to make the purpose of the exercise clear: it will allow the students to explore the released and natural breath unburdened by the tensions we hold as we stand. Though it is about deep relaxation, it is not about actually falling asleep – the students need to attend to the exercise by focusing on the instructions. They may feel relaxed enough to drift off. If that happens, I touch them gently or whisper to them to focus. Take them slowly through the instructions, allowing time for them to fully experience each step. They can lie with legs straight out and feet uncrossed in the supine position; or, if it is easier on the lower back, they can lie with the feet flat and knees up; or they can rest their legs in a chair in the semi-supine position.

Think about space in the torso, large enough for the lungs to inflate fully. Feel space in your hips; breathe deeply as if your breath could carve out more space. Create imaginary space in your knees – send the breath to your knees. Be aware of space in the ankles; imagine you can breathe all the way down to your feet.

o Check in with your breath. Where are you most aware of the breath entering and leaving the body? What is happening in your body as the breath comes in and goes out? Gently place a hand on your center, just below the navel.

o Be aware of the points where your body touches the floor – back of the head, shoulder-blades, hands, hipbones, calves and feet.

o Focus on your breath as it easily enters and leaves your body.

o Let all the air go. Don't force it, just let all the air go on an easy "fff" or "shh", and wait until you feel the need to breathe. When you feel the need, let a breath come in. Don't try to control the length of the inhale or exhale, just let nature and gravity do their things. You should be aware that as you inhale the stomach moves toward the ceiling, and as you exhale the stomach sinks toward the floor. Repeat until this is easy and comfortable. The breath comes in, the breath goes out, and there is a pause.

o Focus your attention on your feet. Allow the feet to feel heavy, letting all the tension drain away into the floor. Picture your ankles as space between your feet and your shins. Imagine that you can breathe into that space. Picture your thighs heavy against the floor. Imagine that all the tension is being drawn into the floor. Be aware of your hips. Picture your hips as space separating your legs from the torso. Imagine that you can fill that space with breath.

○ Go back to your breath. Feel the easy movement of the body as the breath comes in and goes out. Has the breath changed in any way?

○ Focus your attention on your lower abdomen. Let gravity drain all the tension out of that area. Picture your lower spine; feel it lengthen and release toward the floor. Next focus on your belly; let tension drain away into the floor. Breathe into your belly. Picture your whole spine long against the floor. Imagine that the breath can trace the length of your spine.

○ Focus on your shoulders. Feel them wide against the floor. Picture all the tension in your shoulders draining into the floor. Feel your arms heavy as they give in to gravity. Imagine your fingers long and easy as they rest on the floor.

○ Go back to your breath. Focus on the movement in the center of the body. Where do you feel the breath as it enters and leaves the body? Has your experience of the breath changed?

○ Focus your attention on your neck; feel it moving away from the shoulders. Feel the muscles of the neck release. Focus your attention on your head; feel it heavy against the floor. Give your attention to your face. Feel the jaw release. The tongue is like a rug on the floor of your mouth. Feel your lips, cheeks and eyelids go slack.

○ Return to the breath. The breath comes in, the breath goes out, and there is a pause. How has the breath changed? Do you sense more space in the torso? Do you feel the breath more deeply rooted in the lower abdomen?

○ On the exhale say your name: "My name is . . . " Let a breath come in and say your name again. Feel the sound coming from deep inside you. The sound and the breath come from deep in your torso. Commit to the sound as you repeat your name phrase several times.

○ Speak some memorized lines from a monologue or count from one to ten several times. The breath comes in, you speak the text to the end of the thought, and a new breath comes in. In this way connect breath to word and breath to thought. Be aware of anything new in your sound. How does the voice feel when the body is released and the breath is deep?

○ Roll to your side, cradle your head on your arm, and rest there for a couple of breaths. When you are ready, slowly roll up the spine to a standing position. 💿

○ Now that you are standing, realign, ground and center the body. Find the deep central breathing you felt on the floor. Say your name phrase or a few lines of a monologue or count from one to ten.

Discussion questions

What is new in the body? In the breath? How has your experience of the breath changed? What has happened to the voice?

Colin's blog

The group really helped me today by discussing the way that the breathing exercises, the straw, the balloon, and the ones on the mat made them feel. It is reassuring that there is always someone feeling everything, as well as people who really don't feel anything at all during one exercise or another. It makes me feel more normal.

Kristina's blog

There is so much occurring in the body that creates the subconscious breathing – it's mind-boggling what the body naturally knows to do. As we delved further into the mysteries of breath, we lay on the floor and relaxed our bodies and really tried to focus on our breath and the crucial moment that happens before our body expels air. I was really able to deepen and extend the pause. My body was so totally relaxed that I felt like I was connected to all that was happening. My shoulders and jaw were sunk into the floor. When we went to sound, I was amazed at the volume of my voice.

Ribs: releasing the intercostals and connecting to rib swing

We discussed earlier how the ribs have a key function in deep central breathing. They move up and out to create space for the lungs to inflate more fully. The intercostals are muscles between the ribs that allow them to move, making them a flexible cage that surrounds and protects the lungs. As we develop a natural, powerful and expressive voice we want to encourage free and easy rib swing. The following exercises will help you stretch the intercostals and side and back ribs to create more space.

o Find natural alignment, feel the knees release, and keep the back of the neck long and the jaw hanging loose. Raise your right arm up toward the ceiling, feeling the stretch along the exposed ribcage. Pat the ribcage with your left hand vigorously as if patting a pony. Grab the right wrist with the left hand and give a little tug to deepen the stretch. Breathe into the exposed ribcage, feeling the inhale carve out space between each rib.

○ Repeat on the other side.

○ Find a partner. Decide who will be A and who will be B.

A: stand behind B. Place your hands on your partner's ribs, your thumbs by their spine, your fingers wrapping around the lower ribs.

B: exhale strongly on "psht". Then let a full breath come in. Repeat with a strong exhale on "fff" followed by a deep inhale. Find a natural rhythm of the breath cycle, focusing on filling the ribs under your partner's hand with each breath. Repeat ten times.

A: be aware of your partner's rib swing under your hands.

○ Reverse: Partner B hold A's ribcage as A repeats the breathing cycle above.

Discuss with each other what you felt as you held your partner's ribs. How much movement did you feel? Where did you feel it? Did the movement get stronger as the exercise progressed?

For the next sequence lie on the floor or mat.

○ Lie on your right side, prop your head on your arm, bend the knees.

○ Breathe into the exposed ribcage. Feel it move toward the ceiling on the inhale and drop toward the floor on the exhale. Imagine that you can create more space with each breath. Rub the length of your ribcage with your right hand.

○ Gently roll to your stomach. Rest your forehead on the backs of your hands. Breathe into the floor, feel the abdomen press against the floor on the inhale. Feel both ribs move out as you breathe deeply.

○ Gently roll to your left side, prop your head on your arm, bend the knees.

○ Breathe into the exposed ribcage. Feel it move toward the ceiling on the inhale and drop toward the floor on the exhale. Imagine that you can create more space with each breath. Rub the length of your ribcage with your left hand.

○ Gently roll on to your back. Bring the knees to your chest. Let both knees drop easily to the right. Feel the stretch of the lower left ribs. Breathe into the stretch, and hold this position for five deep breaths.

○ Bring the knees back over the chest. Let them drop easily to the left. Feel the stretch in the lower right ribs. Breathe into the stretch, and hold this position for five deep breaths.

○ Slowly and with minimal effort, roll to your stomach, then slowly on to all-fours. Slowly arch the back as high as you can, the head and tailbone moving toward the floor. In yoga this is called "cat back".

○ Reverse the arch so that the belly goes toward the floor, and the head and tailbone lift toward the ceiling. In yoga this is called "cow back".

○ Repeat ten times, breathing in on "cow back" and breathing out on "cat back".

○ Settle back with your bum on your heels, your forehead on the floor (or as close to that position as your flexibility will allow), stretch your arms out along the floor, over your head. In yoga, this is called "child's pose". Breathe deeply into the lower back, imagining that the breath can carve out more space.

○ Roll up the spine to a standing position.

- Go back to your partner. Repeat the partner rib sequence outlined above.

- Give each partner an opportunity to try the voice, focusing on rib swing, either counting one to ten or speaking a few sentences from a monologue.

- Discuss with your partner what changed in the ribs as a result of this sequence.

Discussion questions

What did you discover about rib swing? What changes were you aware of? What happened to the voice? How does awareness of ribs affect the breath?

Kristina's blog

We worked with partners on feeling and observing each other's breathing before and after certain rib stretches. I felt a huge difference in my partner's breathing. She commented on how, previously, my ribcage expanded more on my left side than my right, but after the stretches, it was more even and solid. It was the first time that I really felt my ribcage move up and out; it was a strange yet extremely satisfying feeling.

Colin's blog

The exercise focused on teaching us how to breathe more deeply, while a partner held our ribcage from behind. It was insane – it felt like I was breathing from a much deeper place and thus I could feel my breath taking up my whole torso. Lying on the mats, we focused on filling up and stretching both our lungs. I put my hand on my ribcage and could literally feel my lungs expanding! It was really interesting to hold on to my partner's ribs. It felt as if I could really feel the breath traveling from deep in her diaphragm and making its way up her body and out of her mouth. When we were standing in natural alignment again and spoke our sonnets, my voice was so supported by breath that the words just came out clearly with no effort at all. I also understood what the sonnet meant more deeply than I had before.

Sensing the moment of readiness

This exercise is one you will want to return to over and over and make a part of your daily warm-up. You can do this standing in natural alignment, sitting easily in a chair or lying on the floor. Allow ten minutes the first few times you do this, then five minutes when it becomes part of a daily warm-up.

○ Find the natural rhythm of your breath: the breath comes in, the breath goes out, notice the pause. When that rhythm is deeply established, turn your focus to the moment when the inhale becomes the exhale. Feel it deep in your torso. It may seem like a momentary suspension, an easy change of direction. Stay with this awareness for several breaths.

○ Once you have established the awareness of the moment when the inhale turns to the exhale, mark that point with a gentle "haa". Keep the knees soft, the back of neck long and the jaw released as you sound "haa" each time the inhale becomes the exhale. Repeat at least ten times.

○ Holding the awareness of the moment when the inhale becomes the exhale, lengthen the "haa" so it becomes "haa haa". Repeat several times. Let that evolve into "haa, haa, maa", still focusing on the inhale becoming the exhale.

○ Keep this focus and, with a big space in the mouth, let the sound lengthen to the full extent of the breath, a long "haaaa". Repeat several times until you can feel that perfect moment of readiness – the point in the breath cycle when the inhale becomes the exhale and the body is ready for sound. Memorize what this feels like. Enjoy how easy it is to create full, rich, open sound with so little effort.

○ With the knees still soft, the neck still easy and long, and the jaw still released, change the sound to "hoo" – a long frothy "hoo". Feel it fly from your body; let the sound reach all the way across the room and touch the wall. Keep focusing on the moment when the inhale becomes the exhale. Repeat at least ten times.

○ Change the sound to "heee". Repeat several times, still sensing the moment of readiness when the inhale becomes the exhale.

○ While maintaining the focus on the moment when the inhale becomes the exhale, let the pitches swoop and glide, alternating "haaa", "hooo", "heee". Repeat for at least ten breath cycles.

○ Try some text – four or five lines from a memorized monologue or sonnet. Breathe at thought changes while maintaining the focus on the moment the inhale becomes the exhale.

Discussion questions

What is the moment of readiness like for you? Describe in your own words how it feels. How does this awareness affect the voice? How does the moment of readiness affect your understanding of how the breath works to support the voice?

Reflective voice blog

As breath is so important, I will pause here to let you reflect on the straw, the balloon, abdominal release, the floor breath, rib release, and sensing the moment of readiness. Be specific and address each one. What insights did you have? What questions came up? What sensations did you experience? How did the group contribute to your learning?

Engaging the abdominal muscles

Recoil breath (DVD)

o Say "sh-shhh" with enough power to expel all your air. Feel the recoil of the abdominal muscles as they quickly and naturally release to let the next breath come in. Repeat four times.

o Change the sound to "v-vvv" and repeat four times. Do the same with "z-zzz".

Trampoline breath (DVD)

o Find your natural alignment, grounded and centered. Place a hand gently on your lower abdominal muscles.

o Say "ha ha ha" quickly and lightly as if a little man is using your diaphragm as a trampoline. Repeat the "ha" until you need a breath, then let a breath fall in and repeat three times. Put a hand on your center so you can feel the activation of the transverse muscle. Effort level should be between three and four. Keep your jaw released and the tongue resting on the floor of the mouth.

o Say "hee hee hee" as if that same little man is jumping on the trampoline of your diaphragm. Repeat the sound until you need a breath, then let the breath fall in. Repeat three times.

o Say "ho ho ho" in the same manner as above.

Diamond of support

o Put a finger just below the breastbone. Put another finger just above the pubic bone.

o Say "psht" several times. Notice what is happening in your center. What do your fingers do?

o Now put your hands around your waist, one hand on either side, just below your ribs. Say "psht" again several times. What do your hands do?

At the end of this simple three-exercise sequence, you should feel that your abdominal muscles have been engaged and enlivened. These exercises should be part of your standard daily vocal warm-up.

Building breath capacity and breath management

The following exercises will help you in several ways. First, you gain a kinesthetic or physical understanding of the amount of breath needed for the task. A small task or a short thought requires a smaller breath. A larger task, a bigger emotion, a longer sentence or a larger space require a bigger breath. You will develop the capacity to sustain an even flow of breath to match the length of the thought. In addition, you will increase the flexibility of the breath as you easily move from short to medium to long thoughts.

- Imagine that you are blowing out a single candle. Now imagine that you are blowing out ten candles. Then, blow out a hundred candles.

- Imagine you are holding a feather in your hand. Blow the feather off your hand. Keep the feather in the air with a stream of breath. Blow a handful of feathers across the room. Blow away all the feathers from a huge pillow that has burst open.

- Put your finger to your lips and gently "shush" a talkative movie patron seated a row in front of you. He does not get the message, so "shush" him louder. Then, "shush" him as if to push him out the door with the force of your breath.

Notice that in each case you took the amount of breath necessary to fulfill the requirements of the escalating situation. As the circumstances became more urgent and the need greater, the amount of air taken in and the amount of force behind the released air became larger. (Note: If you begin to feel a little light-headed or dizzy while doing these exercises, take a break until the feeling passes.)

Breath management

This exercise helps your body to learn the lesson of capacity and sustainability from a short thought to a long thought. This time, the thoughts are going to take the form of numbers: one to ten.

- Find easy natural alignment: knees released, back of neck long and soft, jaw released. Say "one". Breathe. Say "one by two". Breathe. Say "one by two by three". Breathe. Continue on in this way to "ten". Be aware of what is happening in the center as you progress. Be aware of the ease of each new breath. The body knows how much breath it needs for the length of the thought coming next. This exercise should become a standard part of your vocal warm-up.

Building capacity and sustainability

○ Stand in natural alignment. Blow out all your air on a "shhhh", and when you need a breath, let one come in. Begin an exhale on "zz". Continue as long as you can comfortably sustain the sound. Don't go on so long that you start to tighten or sputter. Renew the breath, and sustain the "zz" four to six times.

○ You can also do this exercise on "s". Try it both ways and see which sound is easier.

By doing this kind of exercise every day you can double your capacity in a couple of weeks. This should also become a standard part of your vocal warm-up.

Discussion questions

What did you learn about capacity, sustainability and breath management? Which exercises gave you the most easy and natural sense of the breath as it moved in and out of the body?

☉ Up against the wall (DVD)

During the breath exercises it becomes easy to feel connected to deep central breathing, but when we try to connect that with actual acting, it becomes more challenging. Often our habitual physical tensions take over, causing us to lose a sense of connection with the breath. When this happens, I send the actor "up against the wall".

○ Lean your back against the wall, with knees bent. Let your whole body rest, giving your weight into the wall. Head, shoulders and lower back melt into the support of the wall. Find the natural rhythm of the breath deep in your center. Focus on the moment that the inhale becomes the exhale.

○ Speak your monologue, focusing on the breath while releasing your weight into the wall. Breathe at each punctuation mark. Avoid any desire to "act". This is about connecting breath to thought. If emotional connections happen as a result of connecting word to breath, let them happen and go with it.

Spinal breathing

This exercise deepens breath, giving the actor a sense of a more powerful, energized breath rooted in the body. You can start on the floor and work to standing. Allow twenty minutes for the entire sequence.

○ Lie on your back, legs out and feet uncrossed and relaxed. Feel your spine lengthen and your shoulders widen against the floor. Give your weight over to gravity; feel it heavy against the floor. Focus on your breathing.

○ Focus on your tailbone; imagine that breath can reach the tailbone. Breathe all the way to the tailbone.

○ Focus on your kidneys in the lower back; imagine that you can breathe into that area. Feel the lower back alive with breath.

○ Focus on the area between your shoulderblades; imagine that you can breathe into that area. Feel the middle of your shoulders alive with breath.

○ Focus on the base of the skull, where the neck enters your head; imagine that you can send breath to that part of the body. Feel the base of your skull alive with breath.

○ Focus on the crown of the head; imagine that you can breathe into the top of your head. Feel the top of your head alive with breath.

○ Now that you have imagined the major points in your back, imagine that you can draw a breath in through your tailbone that goes all the way up the spine, energizing each of those points. One breath comes in the tailbone and goes up your back to the top of the head, energizing the entire spine.

○ Now focus for a moment on the front of the body. Focus on the middle of the forehead; imagine you can massage that area with breath.

○ Focus on the nose, mouth and chin; imagine that breath can energize your face.

○ Imagine the soft place just beneath the breastbone, the solar plexus; imagine that breath can energize the center of your chest.

○ Focus on your stomach; feel your stomach energized with breath.

○ Focus on your abdomen; imagine that breath can energize that part of the body.

○ Imagine that breath is circular. The inhale comes in the tailbone and energizes the spine, touching each spot that you just so carefully imagined. The exhale goes out from the front of the body – from your forehead, to your face, to your solar plexus, to your stomach, to your abdomen. The circle starts again: inhale up the spine, and exhale down the front of the body. Stay with this until the circular breath is established.

○ Maintaining the specific imagery of the inhale energizing the spine and the exhale traveling down the front of the body, add the sound "ahh" on the outgoing breath. Repeat several times.

○ Now change the sound to "ooh" as the inhale energizes up the spine and exhale travels down the front of the body. Feel the "ooh" sound flowing out from the lips and down the front of the body. Repeat several times.

○ Change the sound to "eee"; continue to be specific with your imagery of the inhale coming in the tailbone and up the spine and the "eee" sound traveling down the front of the body.

○ Change to any vowel, any pitch. Keep the image of the circular breath clear as you let the pitches swoop and glide. Repeat for several minutes.

○ As you continue to engage circular breath, begin to speak your text. At each thought change, take the time to let a new breath enter at the tailbone. Feel the words carried out on the outgoing breath. Feel a space in your mouth that allows the sound all the freedom it needs. Luxuriate with breath and sound; let the text soar into space with no need to control, make sense or perform.

○ When you have finished your monologue, rest for a moment before rolling to your side. Take your time as you prepare to roll up the spine into a standing position.

○ Stand off the mat so your feet are firmly on the floor. If you need to shake or stretch a little after coming off the floor, do so. Ground and center. Reconnect with the spinal breath. Feel the breath come in the tailbone, energize the spine as it travels to the head, and feel the outgoing breath warm the front of the body.

○ When the image of the circular breath is established, add an energized "ahh" on the exhale. Begin with a straight sound that could reach the opposite wall. Feel the power of the spinal breath. Repeat several times.

○ Change the sound to "ooh", letting the pitch swoop and glide. Repeat several times.

○ Change to "eee", and let the pitches swoop and glide. Repeat several times.

○ Use any vowel and any pitch, as if the sound could paint pictures in the air. Feel the breath carry the sound up, down and around. Move with the sound. Paint the room with sound.

○ Add the words of your monologue, still connecting to the image of the circular breath. Paint the room with the words of your monologue.

○ When you have worked through your entire monologue, come to natural alignment, feel your feet against the floor and speak your monologue, allowing it to be whatever it wants to be as a result of the spinal breath sequence.

Discussion questions

Describe what the image of the spinal breathing did for your breath. What changes were you aware of? How did it affect your sound? What new things emerged in the monologue? How do you compare the floor work to the standing work?

Filling the space

Doing breath work in a classroom or studio feels easy and safe. We think we have mastered it. Then we move into the large auditorium where the performance takes place and we suddenly go back to shallow breathing and pressing to achieve the volume required to fill the space. When you transition from small space to large space try this exercise:

o Raise the palm of your hand to about sixteen inches from your face. Breathe that distance and speak several sentences of your monologue to your hand.

o Extend your arm fully and breathe to the tips of your fingers. Speak the monologue to the end of your hand.

o Now focus on the first row of seats. Breathe that distance and speak the monologue to those seats.

o Now look at the center of the auditorium. Breathe that space, feel a little more space in your mouth, and speak to those seats, resisting the temptation to press.

o Now focus on the light booth, all the way at the back of the auditorium. Breathe that distance, and speak your monologue. Resist the temptation to press. Think more space in the mouth, keep the thoughts clear on your lips, and release your knees. If you fill the body with breath and open your mouth you will be able to fill the space with sound without pressing or shouting!

Teacher tip

Breath can be done as a unit of study. Or you can dip in and incorporate several of these exercises into a warm-up or vocal skills class. Some breath exercises should be included in every vocal warm-up.

I have a few tips about dizziness or light-headedness, which happens frequently when doing breath work. Keeping the knees released will help, as can reducing the effort. Opening the eyes and focusing on one hand can steady a wobbly student. Taking a break from the exercise for a few moments may also be helpful.

It is not uncommon for a student to cry during deep breath work. Breathing can release emotions that are tucked away. If that should happen, go to the student,

---

touch him or her gently on the shoulder with a reassuring word or even a hug (you know the level of closeness you have with your students). Tell them it is OK, nothing to be embarrassed about. Then encourage them to sigh, shake out easily, move the face around, and take a little walk around the space. I try to keep them in the room so they don't go out and get locked in that emotional place. Gently help them find their way to a different emotional state. A short discussion with the class may be needed – reinforcing that this can happen, it is not unusual, nothing to be embarrassed about, not something to be joked about or mentioned again outside class. "What happens in voice class stays in voice class." Breathing connects us to who we really are and what we are really feeling. Emotions can be brought up and then replaced by others; we don't have to get stuck there. We are actors; our job is to go to those emotional places and then be able to set the emotion aside at the end of the scene, play, exercise or class. Moving, shaking, stretching, swallowing or sipping water – all can help bring an emotional student back to a steadier place.

Reflective voice blog

Start this entry with the phrase "I write my breath today and it feels . . . " Write for at least one minute without taking your pencil off the page – write continuously, whatever comes up in regard to how your breath feels.

Next, starting with the phrase "What I now know about breath is . . . ", continue to write for three minutes without taking your pencil off the page.

What I want to always remember about breath is

As I continue to develop my voice and breath usage, each time I work on my own practice, I plan to do the following exercises:

Chapter 6 references

For more information on the topics discussed in this chapter refer to:

Boston, Jane, and Cook, Rena, eds, *Breath in Action: The Art of Breath in Vocal and Holistic Practice*. London: Jessica Kinsley Publishers, 2009.

Bunch, Meribeth, *The Dynamics of the Singing Voice*, 4th edn. New York: SpringerWein, 1997.

Carey, David, and Clark Carey, Rebecca, *Vocal Arts Workbook and DVD*. London: Methuen Drama, 2008.

Cook, Rena, "A Week with Andrew Wade", *Shakespeare Around the Globe*. Voice and Speech Review, 2005.

Kayes, Gillyanne, *Singing and the Actor*, 2nd edn. London: A & C Black, 2004.

Lewis, Dennis, *The Tao of Natural Breathing*. San Francisco: Mountain Wind Publishing, 1997.

Linklater, Kristin, *Freeing the Natural Voice*. Hollywood: Drama Publishers, 2006.

Rodenburg, Patsy, *The Actor Speaks*. London: Methuen Drama, 1997.

Speads, Carola, *Ways to Better Breathing*. Rochester: Healing Arts Press, 1992.

Vivier, Judylee, "Inhale, Exhale", *Dramatics Magazine*, Educational Theatre Association, Vol. 78, No. 8 (April 2007).

Exercises

"The Moment of Readiness" is based on work shared with me by David Carey. The "Recoil Breath" and the "Diamond of Support" are based on work shared with me by Gillyanne Kayes.

7

My voice is a trumpet?

How do you know the difference between the sound of a violin, a cello and a stand-up bass? What is it about the quality of the sound that identifies each instrument? How would you describe a trumpet's sound in contrast to a tuba? Can you describe the difference between the voice of James Earl Jones and Fran Dressier of *The Nanny* fame? Or Gwyneth Paltrow and Roseanne Barr? Such descriptions as high or light, smooth or smoky, warm or mellow, piercing or bright might have come to mind. Just as each musical instrument has a distinctive quality, each human voice has attributes that are unique. In addition, the human voice is flexible, changing with emotions, objectives and given circumstances.

It is the actor's task to maximize flexibility and freedom so that the voice can be heard clearly, so it can be warm when called for, stern if necessary, and even ugly in response to the emotional and situational demands of the character.

Your voice and resonance: vibrations that determine quality

A component of vocal quality is **resonance**, the process by which sound created at the vocal folds is amplified, enriched and filtered in the resonating chambers of the body. In a very general way, I think of resonance as disturbed air (breath that has been set in motion by the vocal folds) bouncing around the hollows of the body gaining energy, amplifying some qualities and dampening others. These body hollows make up the **vocal tract**: the throat, the mouth and the sinus cavity. Resonance is your body's natural amplifier.

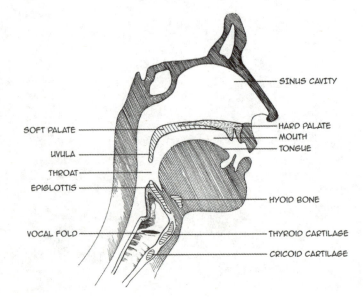

The trombone has a larger, deeper, lower tone than a trumpet. Why? It has a bigger resonating tube. Likewise, the tuba will always have a bigger, deeper sound than the trombone because it has the biggest resonating tube. The throat, mouth and nasal cavities make up the human resonating tube. We have an advantage over brass instruments in that ours is flexible – it can be made longer, shorter, wider or thinner. If you lengthen your neck, you have changed the shape of your vocal tract. If you extend your lips forward, you have changed the shape of your vocal tract. If you smile broadly or close the mouth tightly, you have changed the shape of the vocal tract and will change the quality of your sound. With practice, our resonators can be more free, open, clear, strong, responsive and flexible.

Taking the brass-instrument metaphor a step further, what happens when you put a mute in the end of the trumpet? The sound is muffled. The jaw, tongue and soft palate can be our mutes – dulling, choking and stifling the tone if we let them. Our task then, as actors, is to ensure that our resonators are open and free of tension so we can be loud or soft, beautiful or ugly, warm or strident – whatever our character requires – in a clear, healthy and reliable way.

Each individual has a unique vocal quality. In fact, it is so unique that some security systems have turned to "voice recognition" as a way of ensuring that a person is who they say they are. Our unique qualities are due partly to what nature and genetics have given us in terms of size and shape of mouth, nasal cavities, throat and vocal folds. But a great deal of vocal variety is under our conscious control and can become more flexible with practice. Resonance is an important component of the voice and can be maximized by opening the vocal tract to create space, allowing the vibrating air to be amplified and enriched. More resonance translates to greater vocal ease with more clarity and carrying power that can respond to the changing needs of character and situation. You don't have to be James Earl Jones or Gwyneth Paltrow to have a confident, warm, authoritative or flexible voice. You can practice your way to greater vocal freedom by keeping the jaw released, the tongue forward and down, the soft palate lifted, the throat wide, and the sound moving forward. Then you can claim your spot alongside the actors whose voices you most admire.

In order to maximize resonance, we first need to look at the four parts of the vocal tract: the jaw, the tongue, the soft palate and the throat. All can house hidden tensions which dampen and restrict resonance.

The jaw, in voice terms, is a large hinge that serves as a gate-keeper to aid in the suppression and control of strong emotions; the muscle that opens and closes the jaw is one of the strongest in the body. The effort expended in keeping the jaw rigid results in tension, which backs up into the throat as it stifles or closes off resonance. To maximize space in the throat we need to relax the jaw. It is not about creating a big space at the front of the mouth; it is about releasing the jaw at its hinges, creating space and length between the back molars. The jaw should naturally drop straight down as it opens and releases to gravity. Keep in mind that tendons link the jaw to the throat and finally to the larynx itself.

Tension in the jaw radiates to tension in the vocal folds. If the jaw remains held or tight, the vocal folds will also tighten and constrict, causing them to work harder. The result is fatigue and loss of power, ease and clarity.

The tongue is a huge muscle, often with a mind of its own. We are aware of the front or tip of the tongue because that is what we can see, but the real culprit is the back or root of the tongue. It can carry tension that we are not even aware of, pulling back and down into the throat, muting our sound and dampening clarity and warmth.

The soft palate, which lies at the back edge of the hard palate, has limited mobility but what it has can be maximized. The soft palate also has few nerve endings, so it is harder to feel and challenging to control. A flat or lazy palate can dampen sound and give the voice a nasal quality by allowing air to escape down the nasal cavity. Our goal in voice training is a lifted palate, which creates a big space in the back of the mouth and maximizes oral resonance, which is the sound that carries best in larger spaces.

The throat, located above the vocal folds, is the home of the most insidious of all tensions as it is the most hidden from our view. Its biological function is to constrict and seal the airway to protect us from choking or to help the body, in an emergency, prepare for "fight or flight". There are muscles in the throat that constrict and narrow its opening, even press down on our vocal folds, keeping them from vibrating easily. This area of the throat above the vocal folds is a crucial resonator. In our vocal practice we can learn to retract, widening the upper throat. A big, wide opening translates to open and free sound, sending resonance forward into the space.

I frequently speak of resonance in terms of vibration; when resonance is activated, we feel vibrations in the throat, jaw, face, chest, and sometimes even the top of the head. Our job as speakers is to maximize vibrations and to open our body up to them.

Exercises

The following set of exercises promotes the opening of the vocal tract and the releasing of vibrations, thus maximizing the resonance of the voice.

Jaw

o Clench the jaw and with your fingers find the place where you feel the knot or tightness, rub that spot. Now release the clench and let the jaw hang as you continue to massage at the jaw hinge.

o To further release the jaw, use the heel of the hand to massage the jaw hinge in downward motions. The focus is on releasing the jaw to gravity, not forcing it open. With each pass of the hand, the jaw releases a bit more. Repeat five times at a slow rate of speed, and remember to breathe.

Teacher tip

Though discussing and exercising each of these areas takes a lot of space on the page, the exercises take very little time during an actual warm-up. They should be attended to in each session to serve as gentle reminders to the body: release, open, and free.

○ Take hold of the jaw with both your hands, thumbs underneath, forefingers on top, and open and close the jaw with your hands. Imagine that the jaw is passive, that the hands are doing the work. Remember to keep breathing and maintain a sense of length in the back of the neck.

○ Easily chew in forward circles as if eating very chewy toffee. Do not move the jaw side to side. Think of easy circles that go down and up. Repeat ten times.

○ You might want to sanitize your hands before doing this exercise. Cross your hands at the wrist. Put your thumbs in your mouth and press them against the jaw, that hard spot between your upper and lower molars. Press straight back into that spot. Sustain a medium amount of pressure for at least five seconds. When you release, open and close the jaw to see if an easier space has opened up. This is acupressure for the jaw.

○ Relish the feeling of a loose jaw, released, hanging. Lips can be open or gently closed as long as you maintain a feeling of space.

Tongue

○ While the jaw is hanging loosely, having given in to gravity, shift your focus to the tongue. Be aware that the tongue is resting on the floor of the mouth, gently touching the bottom teeth.

○ Allow the tongue to fall out of the mouth past the lips. Feel it lengthen gently toward the floor. Then stretch it gently toward the ceiling. With tongue still hanging out, send it toward your right ear, then to your left. Allow the tongue to clean the lips gently as if you have just taken a bite from a big juicy peach and you don't want to miss a drop. Clean the inside of your mouth with your tongue.

○ Do a bit of tongue-babble, quickly flicking the tongue against your upper lip (babies do this all the time). Add a couple of great Victorian bows as you tongue-babble.

Tongue-speak

o Continue to let the tongue hang out of your mouth, and count out loud from one to ten, keeping the back of the neck long. Relax the tongue back into the mouth, letting it rest on the floor where it normally does. Count out loud again with a sense of a released jaw and tongue.

o Say a few lines of a monologue in tongue-speak, allowing the tongue to hang loosely out of the mouth. Then speak the same text with the tongue easily back in the mouth.

Be aware of the ease that is created when the tongue and jaw take their rightful places as relaxed articulators and not as tension spots forcing you to create a louder sound artificially.

Soft palate

o Yawn widely with the tongue gently against the bottom teeth. Enjoy the yawn – stretch with the arms as if you have just wakened from a restful night's sleep. Be aware of a huge space opening at the back of the throat. Do this several times to remind the throat that being open and released allows for optimal resonance.

o Sound the consonant "ng". During this sound the tongue and soft palate come together. Feel the point of contact. Release the "ng" into an "ah" and feel the tongue and palate move away from each other. Repeat the following sequence slowly: "ng-gee, ng-gay, ng-gah, ng-go, ng-goo". Feel the tongue and palate coming together on the "ng" and flying apart when you open to the vowel sound.

o Imagine that you have a big, red, juicy apple in your hand. Lift it to your mouth and sink your teeth into it as if to take a large delicious bite. Feel the lift of the soft palate. Repeat and, just before your teeth are ready to sink in, say, "Hello", or perhaps, "Tomorrow and tomorrow and tomorrow". Repeat the bite of the apple, creating a large and easy open space. At the moment of readiness say, "Why fly so high?" or "But soft, what light through yonder window breaks?" or "When shall we three meet again?" You can also use lines from your monologue. On each new breath, lift the imaginary apple as if to bite.

Through this series of exercises you are building an awareness of the lifted soft palate. You are also teaching the soft palate, through muscle memory, the raised position for confident speech that carries effortlessly.

The throat: retraction

When you laugh easily all the muscles in the throat open. Try having a good laugh out loud to see what I mean. Now make the laugh smaller, about a number-four effort level on a scale of one to ten. Next, imagine that you want to laugh but don't want it to show on your face; just feel an inner smile gently retract the throat.

Another easy way to find this sense of opening or retraction is to imagine you are looking at a puppy. What is your instinctive response? You breathe in and sigh out on an "ah". Imagine you are looking at the puppy. Then draw in a breath and before you voice the "ah", feel the throat retracting open. We'll call this the "puppy posture". Which of the two above images works best for you – the inner smile or the puppy posture?

○ On an easy inhale, open the throat with the inner smile or the puppy posture and say, "Tomorrow and tomorrow and tomorrow". Try counting one to ten, or try one of the following phrases: "When shall we three meet again?" "Now is the winter of our discontent."

○ Before each sentence or phrase, breathe in gently and think of the inner smile or puppy posture. You are building a muscle memory of the open and released throat.

○ Try your monologue. On each new inhale, renew the feeling of openness or retraction in the throat.

Humming to increase vibrations

○ Humming is one of the easiest ways to release vibration and increase resonance. Start a comfortably low hum with a big space in the back of the mouth. Hum until you feel the need for a breath, then breathe and start the hum again. Tap gently on the chest to loosen the vibrations. Feel that you can fill your upper chest with vibrations. Keep the back of the neck long and the space in the back of the mouth wide.

○ Raise the pitch a little and continue to hum with a long back of neck and a big space between your back molars. Move the hum around on your face or chew so that the facial muscles are moving the hum around. Explore various pitches in the lower to middle part of the voice as you continue to hum.

○ Blow through the lips on a hum (think of horse lips). Let the pitch vary in small loops as you blow, widening the loops of pitch as you continue to hum. This gathers and increases the strength of vibrations and begins to loosen the pitch range.

○ To bring vibrations forward say "key, key, key, key, key". Speak this on a middle pitch, keeping the back of your neck long. Aim these vibrations on the back of the upper teeth.

○ Intoning is a useful technique that is almost like singing on one note. In this exercise you are going to intone the phrase "My mother makes marmalade": find a pitch in the

93

middle of your range and sing the phrase on the same note, really enjoying the "m" sounds. Then speak it in the same place where you felt the intoning.

○ Next, intone these phrases: "Marv makes my mother merry. My mother may marry Marv." After you intone, speak in the same place you felt the energy of intoning.

○ Finally, take a bit of the monologue you have been working on and intone it. In other words, sing the monologue on one note that is comfortably in the middle of your range. Breathe at the end of each thought until you have intoned the entire monologue. Feel the vibrations forward in your mouth. Then speak the monologue with attention to the spot where you felt the most vibrations while intoning.

◉ T'ai chi sequence (DVD)

This exercise, which is based on a t'ai chi sequence, will use the dowel rods. It contains three basic movements accompanied by a sound progression. Its goal is connecting vibration to breath, waking up the voice easily and fully. It is a warm-up that can be done toward the beginning of each session or at the end to bring all parts of the range on line.

○ Stand in natural alignment with the dowel rod resting easily in front of the thighs. Throughout the exercise, hold the rod easily, keeping shoulders down and neck long.

○ On the inhale, bring the rod to shoulder height. On the exhale, push the rod back down as you sound according to the sound sequence below.

○ Again, on the inhale bring the rod to shoulder height. On the exhale, extend the rod straight out, then down as you sound.

○ Next, on the inhale, bring the rod up and over the head. On the exhale, push the rod straight out and down as you sound.

94

- The sound sequence starts with humming. All three movements – up and down, up and out, and up and over – are done on a hum. The next sequence opens to an "ah". Then, change to "oo", followed by "eee". Finally, advance to any vowel, any pitch.

- A fun variation is "Ninja dowel rods" – any vowel, any pitch and any movement. While sounding, you can move the dowel rods any way you like as long as you don't hit another student. On each inhale, the dowel rod must come back to its original starting position.

⊙ The archer (DVD)

This exercise warms up vibrations and encourages the whole body to open to resonance. It can be done as part of a larger warm-up. As this exercise also focuses the mind and calms performance anxiety, "The archer" is an ideal single warm-up, if time for a full warm-up is not available.

- Widen your base so that feet are further apart, about twenty-four inches. Bend the knees a little, keeping the back straight and the neck long. Cup the left hand easily at the waist; the right arm is across the body with the hand flexed, palm out.

- Exhaling on a hum, the right arm moves to the right across the body, until it is straight to the side. On the inhale, the right hand cups at the waist and the left arm crosses the body.

- Exhaling on a hum, the left arm moves across the body, until it is straight to the side. This movement sequence repeats, sounding the hum four or five times. The sound opens to an "ah", then "oo", then "ee", and finally any vowel, any pitch, repeating the physical sequence five times on each sound.

⊙ Releasing vibrations in the chair (DVD)

Teacher tip

This is a powerful exercise that is best done under your guidance, at least until your students understand what to do and why, at which time it can be done as a partner exercise.

Upper-body tension can murder vibrations. Face, neck, shoulder and upper-back tension stifle resonance. This exercise can help release vibrations and open voices, replacing effort with ease.

o Have a student sit in an armless chair. Ask them to start speaking the monologue. As they are speaking, put your hands on their shoulders, giving a little bit of pressure. Gently massage the shoulder muscles to encourage release.

o Ask them to lean forward with their head hanging between their knees, arms dangling freely, while they continue speaking. Gently pound with cupped palms on their upper back and shoulders, and massage down the arms. Ask them to go to tongue-speak so that all sound feels as if it is flopping easily out the top of the head.

o Continue gently pounding. Then, putting your hand on their lower back, ask them slowly to roll up the spine, continuing in tongue-speak.

o With your hand gently on the spine, follow them up until your hand is at the base of their neck. When they are sitting upright, ask them to let the tongue relax back into their mouth and simply speak.

Usually the sound is quite different. It may be more relaxed, fuller, warmer, clearer or more authentic. Give feedback to the student about what you hear; the other members of the class may be eager to share what changes they hear as well. Ask the student how it feels and to describe what has changed. I come back to this exercise often, until the students get a real sense of how ir feels to speak from this easy and open place. When I am doing individual coaching sessions, I may start with this exercise, then carry on from there. It is like finding true neutral: the clean slate on to which all other acting choices can be layered.

Resonance circle (feeling group vibrations)

The purpose of this exercise is to illustrate the power of sound vibrations – to show in a kinesthetic way that we are physically impacted by resonance. The richer the resonance, the more profound our physical response to it will be.

○ Stand in a circle, with your hands placed gently on the back of the person on either side of you. As a group, begin to sound on a sustained "maa". It doesn't have to be all on the same pitch. Take a breath when you need it and begin the sound again.

○ Explore various pitches, but sustain one pitch per breath. Work as an ensemble to enrich the vibrations.

○ Close your eyes so you are less distracted by the visual. Feel the vibrations on the backs of those next to you. Be aware that you can feel the group vibrations in your entire body.

○ Once the group has established a solid sustained sound, one at a time, move to the center of the circle and feel the vibrations pass through you. Close your eyes once you are in the center and don't be afraid to spend thirty seconds bathing in sound vibrations.

○ When everyone has had time in the center, bring the exercise gently to a close.

Teacher tip

This can be a powerful exercise if the students stay serious and focused. It takes a good bit of time to develop into something really significant. I'd allow at least twenty minutes. If you have a large group, you can have two circles. I generally start the open sustained sound myself to model for them what that sounds like. Don't call it singing, since that can intimidate students who feel they are non-singers – call it sustaining vibrations or intoning. I have also explored using other vowel sounds: ooo, ah, eee. If giggling starts, and it will, coax them to focus on the exercise, close their eyes and listen to the ensemble sound created by the group.

Discussion questions

What was it like to stand in the center of the circle? What happened to the sound as the exercise progressed? What was your experience of the group resonance? Where in your body were you most aware of it? What happened to your own resonance?

☺ Kazoo for forward resonance (DVD)

Forward resonance carries the voice out into space, making it easier to hear from the stage. Many of us let our resonance fall backward, either down the nose or back into the throat. The purpose of this exercise is to feel forward resonance and practice it in a way that will help us carry the sound on to the stage. Deep, dark, chesty, male voices often fall so far back that they don't carry to the stage. Some women's voices can tend to be nasal, a quality that can be unpleasant to our ear and is useful only for a limited range of characters. Another female habit that is growing in popularity is **vocal fry**, which is falling off the voice toward the end of sentences, letting the pitch drop to the bottom of the voice. Though it is heard on television sitcoms and in movies that feature pop culture, it is a voice habit that sends many young women to the speech therapist when they start losing their voices.

For this exercise you will need an inexpensive kazoo – I buy them in bulk from the local party accessories shop.

○ Put the big end of the kazoo in your mouth and hum. You will feel vibrations around the mouth. Hum a tune just for fun – your school song is always a good choice. Now speak a portion of a monologue into the kazoo. Take the kazoo away, and speak the text in the same place you felt the vibrations from the kazoo.

○ Do a whole monologue, one sentence at a time, first with the kazoo and then without, speaking in the same place you felt the energy from the kazoo.

I once had a very talented student who had a terrible case of vocal fry, a habit that she had tried to break for several years. I had her put the kazoo on a string around her neck for an entire semester. Whenever she spoke in vocal fry, either socially or on the stage, I said, "Kazoo it." She would then say the sentence into the kazoo and *voilà*, she was back on voice. If you have any kind of resonance issue, either too far back, in the throat, in the nose, or vocal fry, make the kazoo a part of your personal warm-up every day. It is a quick reminder to your body where healthy, clear, forward resonance should live.

Discussion questions

Describe what the kazoo did for your sound. What is the difference in the voice as you speak text with more forward resonance? How can you incorporate this into your personal practice?

Colin's blog

I loved the jaw sequence. Never before did I realize how much tension I had in my jaw until we actually got in there with our hands and worked it out. I found it really gave me more space in my mouth. In the resonance circle, I could feel every part of my body vibrating. I could feel the back resonance of the two people standing next to me. Standing in the middle of the circle, feeling the vibrations of the group wash over you was amazing. I had no idea that sound vibrations are so real that you can feel them!

Kristina's blog

I discovered that tongue-speak is an excellent way to warm up my mouth and jaw, and that I am far less likely to trip over my words after I have gone through them with my tongue hanging out of my mouth. The more I can be relaxed in the mouth, the more effective my speech, and the more easily vocal and mental patterns flow. Acupressure on the jaw-hinge gave my mouth more horizontal space for the breath and sound to move through. Retracting the throat above the vocal folds was a huge discovery for me both as an actress and as a singer.

Reflective voice blog

Take a few moments to reflect on resonance: what you have learned, where you have questions or confusions, what you have discovered about resonance and your voice. Think about jaw, tongue, soft palate, throat, humming, resonance circle and kazoo. Don't forget to reflect on how the class contributed to your learning.

Resonating energy centers

Teacher tip

This is a meditative exercise which requires maturity and focus; some love it and some find it a bit "new age-y". It is an excellent warm-up for full body resonance and also for deepening the breath and extending the pitch range. It also has a calming effect on the group. The use of color imagery works really well for students who think in color; they grab on to this. For students who don't imagine in color, this aspect can be distracting. I explain this and advise them to use the color suggestions if they find them useful or interesting and to disregard them if they find them distracting.

The purpose of this exercise is to center the breath, encourage vocal vibrations and open the body's receptivity to vocal resonance. This exercise can be done daily or several times a week. It generally takes ten minutes to engage with it fully.

○ Sit in an easily erect position, eyes closed, with a long back of neck, jaw released, and focus on your breath.

○ In your mind's eye, focus on your tailbone and intone the vowel "eh" on a comfortably low pitch, imagining that you can send vibrations to that area. With continued focus on the tailbone, add an image of the color red, as if red vibrations move the sound into and spinning out of the tailbone. Repeat each sound to the end of the breath at least five times.

○ Focus your attention on the space just below the navel; the sound is "o", and the pitch is slightly higher. The color orange is used to inspire vibrations into and spinning out of the abdominal area. Strengthen the vibrations and feel that space come to life from the energy of the sound vibrations. Repeat each sound to the end of the breath at least five times.

○ Next, the focus of attention moves to between the navel and the sternum. The sound is "ow", the color is yellow, and pitch again moves naturally up a tone. Feel vibrations of yellow sound move to and spin out of this area. Repeat each sound to the end of the breath at least five times.

○ The focus now moves to the chest. The sound is "ah", and the color is green. Feel vibrations of green sound move through the chest, lungs and heart. Feel that area come alive with your sound vibrations. Repeat each sound to the end of the breath at least five times.

- Shift the focus to the throat and mouth area; the sound is "oo", and the color is blue. Feel the area come alive with vibrations as the color blue spins though it. Adjust pitch up to maximize vibrations in the throat and mouth. Repeat each sound to the end of the breath at least five times.

- The forehead now becomes the focus; the sound is a hum, and the color is indigo. Adjust your pitch up so you feel vibrations in the forehead. Imagine that the vibrations are streaming out of the forehead. Drill indigo sound-vibrations out through your forehead. Repeat each sound to the end of the breath at least five times.

- The final energy center is the top of the head; the sound "ee" helps to move vibrations into that area. Let the pitch move up as well. The color is violet. Feel the violet sound-vibrations spin out the top of the head – imagine a long stream all the way to the sky. Repeat each sound to the end of the breath at least five times.

- Now let the voice glide easily up and down on any of the above sounds from the tailbone through the top of the head and back again several times. Just let the voice play. Be extravagant as you let the sound motor throughout your pitch range.

- Slowly find your way to standing and to natural alignment. Try a few sentences from a monologue to see if the body is more receptive to the vibrations of the voice, the pitch freer, the sound more released, the breath more deeply rooted in the body.

Discussion questions

What has happened to the breath as a result of this exercise? How would you describe the shifts in your resonance? What did you notice about your pitch range after this exercise?

Reflective voice blog

Review what you have learned about resonance. Which of the above exercises was most useful? Which were not so helpful? What did you learn about your own voice through this chapter? What will you try to take on as part of your personal voice practice?

Teacher tip

Often during the resonance exercises, I have the students use a Shakespeare sonnet of their choice. The sonnets lend themselves easily to this kind of work and the length is manageable. It might be helpful for you to bring in some of the more accessible sonnets for them to choose from (go to www.sonnetsofshakespeare.com). Here are some, by number, that I have found to be accessible: 2, 12, 17, 18, 27, 29, 57, 65, 71, 116 and 130.

When they have the sonnet memorized, and often after the resonance circle, I go directly into the "Sonnet Walk". This provides an opportunity for each to speak their sonnet aloud without the pressure of a performance. They all begin to walk purposefully through the space. When one decides s/he is ready to speak their sonnet, they begin. The rest of the class stops and gives full attention. When the speaker finishes the sonnet, they begin walking again until another student begins to speak. If two begin at the same time, one stops to let the other continue. This seldom happens, though, because they are tuned in to the group and begin to sense who is ready to speak. The walk continues until all have said their sonnets. Sometimes, if the group feels tentative, I tell them I will start. I walk with them and am the first to speak. I model how to stop and give attention to the speaker and how to begin walking again with purpose. The exercise generates energy and confidence. It also gives you an opportunity to hear how their voices are developing. The sonnet walk or monologue walk can happen at any point in the process. I come back to it frequently.

Chapter 7 references

For more information on the topics discussed in this chapter refer to:

Barton, Robert, and Dal Vera, Rocco, *Voice Onstage and Off*, 2nd edn. New York and Oxford: Routledge, 2011.

Bunch, Meribeth, *The Dynamics of the Singing Voice*, 4th edn. New York: SpringerWein, 1997.

Carey, David, and Clark Carey, Rebecca, *Vocal Arts Workbook and DVD*. London: Methuen Drama, 2008.

Kayes, Gillyanne, *Singing and the Actor*, 2nd edn. London: A & C Black, 2004.

Linklater, Kristin, *Freeing the Natural Voice*. Hollywood: Drama Publishers, 2006.

Rodenburg, Patsy, *The Actor Speaks*. London: Methuen Drama, 1997.

Exercises

Palate work and retraction were adapted from the work of Gillyanne Kayes. "T'ai chi with Dowel Rods" and "The Archer" are based on work first shared with me by David Carey. "Kazoo for Forward Resonance" was first shared with me by Kate DeVore.

8 The highs and lows of voice

Pitch – the highs and lows of the voice – is so important in the vocal development process that there is a whole chapter devoted to its understanding and integration. We may understand the concept of pitch better in musical terms as a note being high or low. Although the speaking voice does not sustain pitch as in sung music, pitch is always present. Highness or lowness here is not to be confused with loudness or softness, which have to do with volume. **Pitch range** is the distance from the highest note to the lowest note that an individual voice can use – it is a range of pitches that an actor has at his disposal. It is sad but true that most of us use only a few notes of pitch variety in our stage work, and even fewer in our everyday speech. Most of those notes generally sit in the lower third of our actual pitch range. The developed voice can have up to two octaves, or fourteen notes, of usable pitch range. This is not to say we should use all fourteen within every utterance, but the more dynamic highs and lows should be easily available when required by the needs of the speech, scene or space.

Pitch is the result of tension, or degree of stretch, in the vocal folds themselves. The more stretched the folds, the higher the sound; the more relaxed the folds, the lower the sound. Think of the strings on a guitar: the fatter, looser strings have lower tones, while the smaller, tighter strings have higher tones. The relative amount of stretch or looseness in the vocal folds is controlled by the arytenoids in the larynx that move back to stretch the folds for higher pitches or bend forward to bunch or loosen the folds for lower pitches, just like a rubber band wrapped around your thumb and forefinger.

We only have to think of the monotone teacher whose lecture drones on with no pitch variety to know that one-note communication puts us to sleep. The teacher who uses her full voice and pitch range to express her enthusiasm and knowledge of her subject engages and holds us. Think for a moment about your favorite teachers. What is it about their voice that keeps you interested, that draws you into their voice and their message? I bet that part of their success has to do with an expressive voice that makes use of a wider pitch range than most.

In our contemporary relaxed culture, it is cool to sit vocally at the bottom of the range, to speak in our lowest notes. Young men often try to sound more manly, so they force the voice down into what they think is a more masculine range. Young women want to be taken seriously or sound sexy so they use their lowest notes as well. There are, by contrast, some young women who keep their "little girl" voice long after they have grown beyond that physically. Perhaps for psychological reasons, they are hanging on to past behaviors and relationship patterns that feel comfortable. Using either extreme of the pitch range scale is not as effective for the actor because it limits expressive options, limits the ability to be heard and understood in larger spaces, and can lead to vocal health issues where loss of voice can become a real possibility.

We can expand our pitch range in a number of ways. These exercises are fun, quick and can add zest to a warm-up, while extending your pitch range at the same time! Do the following exercises in the middle of your warm-up, after the voice has been motoring comfortably.

Teacher tip

If a student is really trapped in either extreme of the pitch range, these exercises may not yield immediate results. They need to be worked as part of the daily warm-up. Eventually the range will start to loosen up, and more notes will be available. This is gradual work that encourages trust in the process. Notice below I talk in terms of "high-ish, low-ish" – students should ease the voice, not force it to places that cause it to feel scratched or fatigued.

Exercises

Ng siren

○ On the "ng" sound, make a tiny baby or puppy whine, repeat easily several times.

○ Stay on "ng" as you begin to siren in ever expanding loops of pitch – high-ish to low-ish, not highest to lowest – easing your voice into higher and lower places.

○ Change to an "eee" siren, again in loops of pitch that go from high-ish to low-ish notes. Keep knees soft, back of neck long and remember to breathe.

○ Change to an "ooh" sound, letting pitches swoop and glide. You might at this point want to add movement; as the pitch goes up the body goes up, and as the pitch goes down the body goes down – *à la* Martha Graham, the modern dancer.

○ Expand to any vowel, any pitch. Be extravagant as you explore swoops and glides, and let your body follow. There is no right or wrong – just enjoy the pitch and body moving together.

⊚ Pitch absurd (DVD)

○ Choose any sonnet or monologue and speak it in pitch absurd – that is letting the pitch move up and down extravagantly, randomly, using pitch extremes, regardless of content or meaning. If moving physically a bit helps you and your voice stay released, then move as well.

o When you have done the whole monologue in pitch absurd, find natural alignment, release knees, keep back of neck long, breathe, and speak the monologue, letting the pitch go where it naturally wants to go.

Discussion questions

Describe how your pitch range reacted to these exercises. What are the changes you noticed? What places in your range seemed to be more comfortable and flowed more easily? Did any parts feel creaky or unnatural? What happened to the monologue after the pitch-absurd exercise?

High/low

Below are two lists of contrasting words. The first word in each pair inspires a higher note. The second word feels as if it needs to be spoken on a lower note. Physicalize, letting the body go up as pitch goes up and down as pitch goes down. Have fun – do this with flair!

High	Low
Light	Dark
Sweet	Sour
Happy	Sad
Success	Failure
Laughter	Tears
Friend	Foe
Love	Hate
Joy	Sorrow
Generous	Miserly
Tickled	Tormented
Freezing	Melting
Healthy	Sickly
Rich	Poor
Reward	Punish
Win	Lose

Optimum pitch, sometimes called center note, is the note around which our voice is the clearest, easiest, most efficient, and resonant. Optimum pitch also has more carrying power than any other place in your pitch range. Most of my students find that their optimum pitch is higher than they think it should be; a few young women find that it is lower than they think it is. In any case, learning to use optimum pitch on stage and even in social speaking is one of the best things you can do for the health, efficiency and expressivity of your voice.

What follows are four ways to find your optimum pitch and strategies to help you integrate optimum pitch into your stage and social voice.

⊙ Pringles tube (DVD)

For this exercise you will need an empty Pringles tube.

○ Hold the Pringles tube gently between your thumb and fingers and bring it close to your mouth, almost but not quite touching your lips. Vocalize in the tube, starting from your lowest comfortable note on an "ah". Give the sound the energy of effort level four or five. Then vocalize up a tone at a time, until you feel a change in the tube. When you reach your optimum pitch, the tube will vibrate in your hand, and you will sound noticeably louder. Not magic – the tube is a biofeedback tool that amplifies your optimum pitch: it feeds back to you your best resonant sound.

○ Once you find your optimum pitch, speak your full name on that pitch, "My name is . . . and this is my optimum pitch." If you lose it, go back to the tube and find it again. Once you can speak your name at that pitch, try a few sentences of a monologue. Go back to the tube as often as you need to.

○ Try working with a partner. Vocalize in the tube, then let your partner listen for the change in the resonance. Sometimes a partner can hear our optimum pitch better than we can. Try speaking your name and a few lines of text. Let your partner feed back what they hear. How is this different from what they usually hear or different from how you usually sound?

○ Reverse and let your partner have a go with the tube and optimum pitch.

One to ten – shoot for the middle

Count out loud one to ten – the odd numbers high-ish in your range, the even numbers low-ish in your range. Keep the back of the neck long and don't lead with your chin. Once you have counted to ten, without thinking, planning or judging, shoot for the middle note and say "My name is . . . and this is my optimum pitch." Then speak a few lines of text.

Five from the bottom

○ Find your lowest comfortable note, vocalize on "ah" and move up five notes. That should be your optimum pitch. Say "My name is . . . and this is my optimum pitch." Try a few lines of text.

Uh-huh

○ A quick way to access optimum pitch is to find your authentic "uh-huh", the second note of which is usually your optimum pitch. I use this one sometimes when I am doing voice-over work and I feel my pitch is sitting on the bottom of my voice. I need to bring the voice back to its "sweet spot" quickly. I speak an "uh-huh" and the second note of that is my optimum pitch!

○ To help a partner find their authentic "uh-huh", ask an obvious question, like, "Are you wearing jeans today?" To which your partner answers, "Uh-huh" Take whatever that second note happens to be and go right on to speaking, "I am . . . and this is my optimum pitch."

Curing falling inflection disease

Falling off the ends of sentences is a serious problem for many young actors. It is a usage habit that can be quickly cured with a couple of simple techniques. Those of you who are frequent offenders have no doubt been told by your director or drama teacher to lift the ends of your sentences. You have no doubt tried. Consciously trying to fix the problem generally leads to unnatural punching or pressing. These exercises let you feel the lift and the forward moving energy from thought to thought naturally. Do these exercises as many times as it takes until your body learns this lesson.

○ **Toss the ball**   Hold a tennis ball in your hand. On the last word of each sentence, toss the ball up.

○ **Kick the box**   Put an empty cardboard box on the floor in front of you. On the last word of each sentence, kick the box.

○ **Final word**   Physicalize the last word of each sentence, or present the final word on your hand as if to give a gift.

Colin's blog

Of all the ways to find optimum pitch, the Pringles tube worked best for me, and I could quickly and easily find the note. I found that my optimum pitch was a little higher than my normal speaking voice. It was actually very easy and comfortable for me to speak on that pitch and it feels very healthy too. This exercise was really valuable as I can take it with me and apply it to my voice work in other situations.

Kristina's blog

To find our optimum pitch we held a Pringles can almost touching our lips. The first try, I started way too high, so it didn't work. So then I started from my low note and went up – it worked! My optimum pitch is lower than the pitch at which I normally speak, which was different from the rest of the class. I honestly wish that I had learned how to find optimum pitch years earlier.

Discussion questions

How is optimum pitch different from your habitual pitch? How does it feel? Where, specifically, do you feel the changes in your voice?

Teacher tip

Many students freak out when they find that their optimum pitch is higher than they think it should be. Men of course don't want to sound less masculine, and women don't want to sound like little girls. I then demonstrate the power of resonance. I can speak at my optimum pitch without full resonance and indeed sound like a little girl. When I engage the full complement of resonators at the same pitch previously used, I sound like a woman with a clear, easy voice. I use at least one of these optimum pitch exercises with every warm-up until it becomes a natural, usable tool to access the students' most efficient, clear and expressive sound.

⊛ Master thespian (DVD)

Another range-extending exercise is "Master thespian" which, like "Pitch absurd", encourages the actor to be extravagant vocally and physically. It is inspired by an old *Saturday Night Live* skit in which actors Jon Lovitz and John Lithgow dressed as ambitious and egomaniacal Shakespearean actors and overacted outrageously, voicing and physicalizing in a broad, stereotypical way, mocking acting styles of that period.

○ Choose a monologue that you would like to work with and play "Master thespian", with my permission to overact totally. Use extravagance of physicality, pitch range and qualities, paying no heed to character consistency.

○ When you have finished the entire monologue, find natural alignment, ground, center, breathe and say the monologue, allowing it to be whatever it is, as influenced by the previous exploration.

Discussion questions

How did that exercise shake up your pitch patterns? What new qualities did you discover in the monologue? What new physical information did you receive about the monologue?

Reflective voice blog

Consider the work you have done with pitch range, optimum pitch, "Pitch absurd", and "Master thespian". What discoveries did you make about your habitual use of pitch and pitch range? What questions were raised? What discoveries did you make? How might you integrate this new knowledge into your daily practice?

Chapter 8 references

For more information on the topics discussed in this chapter refer to:

Barton, Robert, and Dal Vera, Rocco, *Voice Onstage and Off*, 2nd edn. New York and Oxford: Routledge, 2011.
Carey, David, and Clark Carey, Rebecca, *Vocal Arts Workbook and DVD*. London: Methuen Drama, 2008.
Rodenburg, Patsy, *The Actor Speaks*. London: Methuen Drama, 1997.

Exercises

'Ng Siren' was first shared with me by Gillyanne Kayes. "Pringles Tube" for optimum pitch was first shared with me by David Carey. "Pitch Absurd" was first introduced to me by Patsy Rodenburg.

9

No, I don't have marbles in my mouth

Articulation, consonants!! Articulation, consonants!! This is the battle cry of all directors. In your most connected moments of acting, you hear shouted from the back row, "I can't hear you!" "I can't understand you!" Yes, it is a reality of our acting lives; we understand that we can't always be understood. Now, what are we going to do about it? Can we change, "Articulation, consonants!!" to, "Thank you so much, I heard every word"? Can we get the marbles out of our mouths? Yes, we can!

It might be helpful here to give a little background on why clarity is such a sticking point for young actors. As I have mentioned several times in this book, the casual nature of contemporary culture leads us to casual speech. With casual speech comes a mouth that doesn't want to open; thus, vowels are not given ample space. If we are using "contemporary casual speak", the articulators – lips, teeth, tongue, palate – don't want to come together in an energized way; they approach each other but don't really want to shake hands, as it were. "Falling inflection disease" is rampant in American speech: falling off the ends of sentences both in volume and clarity is so ingrained in our speaking and in our hearing that we often don't notice when we fail to finish sentences! Our thought energy trails off in the assumption that our listeners already know what we are going to say, so why bother to finish anyway?

An important word here about dialect: General American is one that will be called for in many play scripts and one that all actors need to be able to use with fluency when the role requires it. But this does not imply that General American is more proper or standard and that other dialects are somehow sub-standard. More importantly, if you speak a dialect other than General American you are not required to change your personal dialect in order to be successful. You speak the way you speak and that reflects where you have come from and who you are. Our goal as we study speech is to gain flexibility, ease and clarity, so we can adapt to the requirements of the role or production. In social or professional situations we always need the capacity to be clear and understood. Neither of these requires that we all speak a common dialect that makes us all sound the same.

This chapter deals with the subject of speech, which includes:

○ articulation of consonants

○ fully formed vowels and diphthongs

○ flexible and responsive articulators

○ clarity of thought

We will look at each topic to make sure we know what it is and what it entails, do some exercises that train muscles, and explore how this can be applied to acting.

> **Teacher tip**
> *My guess is that students will not go through this chapter by themselves. As crucial as speech work is to being able to hear your high-school actors on stage, they simply will not take the time to slog through the detail. You will have to guide them through. The chapter is laid out in a highly systematic and sequential way. I have tried to make what can be very daunting as straightforward, active, experiential and fun as possible. Be their guide and you will see results in understanding and a raised commitment to clarity of speech.*

Phonetics is the science or study of speech sounds. Now, for me, anything that has the word science in the definition sets off all kinds of warning bells in my artistic right brain: "for left brains only – this cannot be fun". However, I have found that a little phonetics work in the pursuit of understanding consonants and vowels can help actors speak more clearly and engage with language in a more dynamic way. Western spoken languages are made up of two major sound categories: **consonants** and **vowels**. In the General American dialect alone there are twenty-four consonants and nineteen vowels and diphthongs. It helps to have an awareness of each sound, how and where in the mouth it is formed. These sounds are literally made all over the mouth, and the mouth needs to be working harder for stage speech than it typically does for social interactions. Through awareness and practice, these sounds become more specific, clear and emotionally engaging. It may be interesting, through our study of consonants and vowels, to discuss and demonstrate how these sounds differ in the other dialects that make up the tapestry of your group.

You will notice in the illustration of the speech organs: the articulators, which include the lips, teeth, tongue, palate, soft palate. Each of these needs to be exercised and sensitized to the specificity required for clear speech. A brief, mindless tongue-twister, which is what many articulation warm-ups consist of, is not enough to train the mouth to engage fully with the many small but crucial bits of language called for in theatrical dialogue.

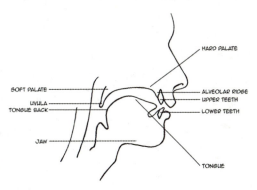

Consonants

What are consonants? Everything that is not a vowel! Yes, of course, but much more than that. Defined, a **consonant** is an obstruction of air flow. Back to the breath – air is flowing, the vocal folds are oscillating and creating tiny puffs of disturbed air. That stream of air is obstructed in some way by the articulators and we have created a sound we know as a consonant. We can talk about consonants in three ways:

○ How they are formed: that is the **manner of articulation**.

○ Where in the mouth they are formed: that is the **place of articulation**.

○ Whether they are **voiced** or **voiceless**.

Manner of articulation

Plosives: consonants formed by a total obstruction of air followed by a release that creates a popping noise:

   p   b   t   d   k   g

Say each of these six plosives several times, feeling the *energy* of the total obstruction of air and the *joy* of the release that creates a popping noise. Commit totally to the sound in each case.

Fricatives: consonants that are formed by a partial obstruction of air, creating a continual hissing sound:

   f   v   th (as in **thin**)   *th* (as in **these**)   *s   z   sh   j* (as in beige)   *h*

Say each of these nine fricatives several times, feeling the *energy* and *joy* of the vibrations of the partially obstructed air flow as you sustain the sound. Commit totally to the sound in each case.

Affricates: consonants that are formed by a complete obstruction released into a partial sustained obstruction – in other words, a plosive followed by a fricative.

   dj as in the word **judge** or **jump**   *ch* as in the word **church** or **chair**

Say each of these affricates several times, feeling the *energy* and *joy* of the complete obstruction followed by the partial release. Commit totally to the sound in each case.

Nasals: consonants that are formed by air escaping down the nasal cavities.

   m   n   ng

Say each of these nasal consonants several times, feeling the *energy* and *joy* of the vibrations you feel in the nasal cavities. Commit totally to the sound in each case.

Approximants: consonants that are formed when the surfaces of two articulators move toward each other and move away before they actually touch.

r   *y* (as in the word **y**es)   *w*

As you say these sounds feel the surfaces that come close together and then enjoy their movement apart.

Lateral approximants: one consonant is formed with air escaping from two sides of the tongue.

l (as in the word **l**eft)

Say this sound feeling the tip of the tongue solidly on the alveolar ridge and enjoy the feeling of the air escaping out of the sides of the tongue.

Place of articulation

Consonants can be formed in the following places in the mouth:

○ The lips

○ The lips and teeth

○ The teeth

○ The alveolar ridge

○ Post-alveolar ridge

○ Palate

○ Soft palate

○ Uvula

Exercise

Using a small hand mirror, look at your mouth:

○ Look at your **lips**. Bring them together, making a popping noise as they come apart. How many different sounds can you make with your two lips?

○ What consonants can be made with your two **lips**?

p   b   m

Try these sounds several times, energetically bringing the lips together and feeling them fly apart with the force of the breath. Look at your lips in the mirror as you do this.

○ Again using the hand mirror, watch your teeth and lips explore sound together. How many sounds can be made by your lips and teeth working together? You don't have to limit yourself to just recognizable speech sounds.

○ What consonants can be made with the lips and the teeth?

f   v

Try these sounds several times, energetically bringing the lips and teeth together and feel the energy of the air hissing through.

○ Find your **alveolar ridge** in the mirror. It is the hard ridge just behind the top front teeth. How many sounds can be made on the alveolar ridge? You don't have to limit yourself to recognizable speech sounds.

○ What consonants can be made with the tongue against the alveolar ridge?

t   d   n   r   s   z   l

Try these sounds several times, energetically bringing the tongue to the alveolar ridge. Notice the energy it takes to fully articulate these sounds.

○ Still with the mirror, look just behind the alveolar ridge, that small bit that starts up toward the hard palate, called the post-alveolar. Let your tongue find that small area. Explore the sound possibilities that can be created at the post-alveolar.

○ What consonants can be created with the tongue on the post-alveolar?

sh   j   (bei**g**e)

○ Contrast the difference between **s** and **sh**. Notice how the tongue slightly shifts from alveolar ridge on "s" to post-alveolar on "sh".

○ In your mirror, look at your **hard palate**, way in the top of your mouth. Let your tongue explore the whole expanse of that huge area. Explore how many different sounds you can make with tongue against the palate.

What sounds can be made on the hard palate? There are a number of human voice sounds that can be made on the palate.

○ Return to your mirror, and find your **soft palate**, also called the **velum**. Explore the different kinds of sounds that can be made on the soft palate. You may find that other parts of your tongue are contacting the velum to make new sounds. The tip of the tongue is not so active now, as most of the work is done with the back of the tongue. What are the consonants you make on the soft palate?

> *k*   *g*   *ng*

Using the mirror, watch yourself as you energetically form these consonants.

○ Again, with your mirror, look as far back in your throat as you can to find that "hangy-down thing" called the **uvula**. It can move up and down pretty dramatically. Try lifting the soft palate as you learned to do in Chapter 4 and see what the range of movement up and down is for the uvula. It also comes in different shapes and sizes. Take a moment to look at some of the uvulas of your friends sitting next to you. You will notice there is a wide variety of shapes and sizes. What sounds can you make with the uvula? Do any of them sound recognizable to the General American dialect? If you speak French, German or Israeli, some of these sounds may feel familiar.

Now that we have explored consonants in regard to the **manner of articulation** and **place of articulation**, let's look at the final way we can identify one consonant from another.

Voiced or voiceless

The last way we can define consonants is whether they are voiced or voiceless. This refers to the presence or absence of vibrations at the vocal fold level. Take, for example, *p* and *b*. Put two fingers gently on your larynx, say first *p*, then *b*. On which sound do you feel more vibration under your fingers? You probably said *b*. We call the *b* voiced because you are voic-ing vibrations at the vocal folds; *p* is voiceless because there are no vibrations at the vocal folds.

> Try *f*   *v*   *s*   *z*,
> *th* as in **th**in and *th* as in **th**ese,
> *ch* as in **ch**air
> and *dj* as in **j**ump.

Which are voiced and which are voiceless?

In conclusion, we have talked about the three ways we can define consonants: **manner of articulation, place of articulation** and whether or not they are **voiced** or **voiceless**.

The ever-changing "r"

The "r" is a sound that can vary widely from dialect to dialect or within a single dialect. In Spanish, Italian or Scottish, the "r" can be trilled or tapped. In French or German, the "r" is pronounced on the uvula. In General American "r" is called a retroflex because the tip of the tongue curls toward the palate. In East Indian dialect the underside of the tip of the tongue contacts the palate. The standard British "r" is sometimes not sounded at all. What "r" pronunciations can you do? If General American is not your first dialect, how do you pronounce the "r"?

Exercises

Consonant conga

○ Speak the consonants below eight times each with a steady hip-hop rhythm, moving freely in response to the rhythm:

> *p   b   t   d   k   g   f   v   th   th*
> *s   z   dj   ch   m   n   ng   l   w*

○ Bring the consonant conga to a conclusion with a luscious "mmmm" that you experience throughout the body.

Plosives

○ Repeat the following voiceless plosives several times, feeling the energy of each sound.

puu tee kaa   puu tee kaa   puu tee kaa   puu tee kaa

○ Repeat the following voiced plosives several times, feeling the energy of each sound.

buh dah geh dah   buh dah geh dah   buh dah geh dah   buh dah geh dah

Consonant drills

○ Repeat the following phrases several times at a three- or four-volume level (too much volume effort on consonant drills can cause overwork at the vocal folds). Enjoy the full energy of the consonants, particularly final consonants. Really wrap your mouth around them, using more muscularity than you normally would.

Unique New York, unique New York, you know you need unique New York.

Big black bugs brought buckets of Black Beard's blood.

Red leather, yellow leather.

My mother makes marmalade to make Marv merry.

A skunk sat on a stump
The skunk said the stump stunk
And the stump said the skunk stunk.

Let us go together to gather lettuce
Whether the weather will let us or no.

Five frantic fat frogs fled from fifty fierce fishes.

Cheryl's cheap chip shop sells cheap chips.

If a hairnet could net hair,
How much hair could that hairnet net,
If a hairnet could net hair?

Mouthing

Choose a monologue that you are working on and mouth the entire speech; that is, really use the articulators, but create no sound. Fully engage the lips, teeth, tongue and palate, as if you want a person across the room to read your lips but you dare not utter a sound. When you have completed mouthing the entire text, speak the text on voice, paying as much attention to the articulators as you did when you mouthed.

Every part of every word

Speak another monologue at volume-level two, slowly pronouncing every part of every word, every tiny syllable, every middle and final consonant. When you have finished the entire speech, speak at normal pace and volume level.

Discussion questions

What have you discovered about consonants and clarity through these exercises? What has changed in your delivery of the monologues? How can you take this awareness into your daily personal practice?

Reflective voice blog

Write about your experiences with the consonant work: discoveries, questions and things you will include in your personal practice.

Teacher tip

I have noticed an increase in problems with the "s" consonant in young actors. This includes the whistling "s", slushy "s", lisps and tongue-thrusts. To oversimplify, this is caused by excess tension in the tongue-tip as the "s" is formed, or the tongue coming too far forward. To effect a change in this usage habit takes daily practice, often with a speech therapist. I have found a CD created by Ginny Kopf, called "The S Drill" very helpful. It is available at www.voiceandspeechtraining.com from Voice Print Publishing. An "s" issue is a speech habit that can limit casting opportunities. It can be lessened or eliminated with consistent daily practice, and the sooner a young actor begins working on it the better.

Vowels

I chose to start our speech discussion with consonants, but of course that is only half the picture. Vowels are the other branch of clear and expressive speech. If consonants are the bones of speech, then vowels are the heart and soul. Some say that while consonants carry the clarity of meaning, vowels impart the emotional content. I have observed that both vowels and consonants must be fully realized for speech to be clear to the ear and piercing to the heart.

So what are vowels? How do we define them? How do we distinguish one vowel sound from another? Let's start with the broad definition: **vowels** are unobstructed air – that is, air passing through the vocal folds straight out an open mouth.

Long vowels

Let's look first at long vowels. These are vowels that sustain for a period of time.

ee as in **e**at   ah as in f**a**ther   oo as in g**oo**se

If they are all created by unobstructed air, how do we know one of these vowel sounds from the others? *Something must happen within the mouth to change the shape of the sound.*

❍ Say a good loud and long *ee*. Describe what is happening in the mouth. Where is the tongue? Let's get even more specific: where is the tip of the tongue? Where is the back of the tongue? Where do you feel the most energy or engagement in the tongue? What is the size of the opening of the mouth? More closed than open?

Perhaps you found that for the *ee*, the tongue is close to the roof of the mouth, that the front of the tongue is most active. The space in the mouth is more closed than open.

❍ Now say a good loud and long *ah* as in "father". Where is the tongue now? Where do you feel the energy in the tongue? What part of the tongue feels more active on this vowel? What is the size of the opening? Where is the tongue in relation to the roof of the mouth? How is this set-up different from the *ee*?

Perhaps you found that for *ah* the tongue is low in the mouth, as far away from the roof of the mouth as it can get – it is an open vowel. The back of the tongue is more active or engaged. So *ah* is an open, back vowel.

In just these two examples, we have isolated two changes that happen in the mouth to turn one vowel to another:

1) Considering the position of the tongue in the mouth: **how close** it is to the roof of the mouth or **how open** it is from the roof of the mouth. We can identify a vowel sound by the tongue's position in relation to the roof of the mouth.

2) **Which part of the tongue is most active**? Or where do we feel the most engagement in the tongue on a certain vowel: the **front**, **middle** or **back**? In our examples above, for *ee* we felt that the tongue was most engaged at the front. For *ah*, the back of the tongue was engaged.

Exercises

○ Try the long vowels, repeating each several times with energy, and try to sense whether the tongue is open or close and what part of the tongue is active.

ee as in **e**at   ah as in f**a**ther   oo as in g**oo**se

Lip rounding

What did you notice about the lips on *oo*? There is some lip rounding that starts on those back vowels. So **presence or absence of lip rounding** is the third and final marker in defining vowels.

⊙ Vowel dance (DVD)

○ For this exercise, the group will need to spread out in the space so they can move freely. Taking each long vowel one at a time, think it, breathe it and speak it over and over, quietly at first, then gaining energy and strength. Let the vowel begin to move you through space. Explore pitch, levels and length as you fully experience each vowel before moving on to the next.

ee   ah   oo

Observe how the different vowel sounds evoke different qualities of sound, movement and feeling.

Short vowels

In contrast to the long vowels, we also have short vowels that are quicker in duration.

i as in k**i**t   eh as in **e**very   uh as in str**u**t   u as in p**u**t

○ After you have said the vowel within the context of the sample word, isolate each short vowel, feel its quick, incisive energy.

k**i**t: How close is the tongue to the roof of the mouth? Where do you feel the most engagement in the tongue? If you said that the tongue is close and the front of tongue is active, you are right. Did you observe that it is not as close as *ee* and the tip of the tongue is not as tense?

○ Spread out in the space and repeat the vowel dance, this time contrasting the short and long vowels. Randomly let the vowels move you, going from long to short and back again. Feel the difference in the quality of sound, the length of sound, the pitches, levels and feelings that are evoked by each sound.

Diphthongs

Diphthongs are two vowels that are spoken as one sound. There are five in General American dialect. As you speak the words below, pay close attention to the diphthongs in **bold** type, and feel the blending of the two vowels to form one.

ay as in f**a**ce   *i* as in pr**i**ce   *oy* as in ch**oi**ce

o as in g**o**at   *au* as in m**ou**th

Diphthongs typically vary a good bit from dialect to dialect. If you speak English with a regional dialect such as Texas/Oklahoma or an accent like Spanish, you may want to discuss and demonstrate how these sounds change in your dialect.

Physicalize the diphthongs

○ On a copy of a short monologue, circle all the words that contain diphthongs. You might need help at first to be able to see a word and know that it contains one of the sounds you are looking for. You can work on this with a partner if you like.

○ Once you have circled all the words containing diphthongs, spread out in the space and read your text out loud. Each time you get to a circled word, physicalize it extravagantly, with no regard for literal meaning. When you have read the entire monologue and physicalized the diphthong words, stop. Find natural alignment, breathe and speak the monologue. See if the diphthong words have changed the speech in any way.

Vowels only

○ Using the same monologue you used for the mouthing exercise, speak only the vowels and diphthongs, eliminating all consonants. Do this easily, letting the vowels flow one into the other, avoiding choppy glottal attacks. Don't worry about getting each one perfectly in order; speak the essence of the vowels, using a kind of "soupy", free-form modern dance rendition. I find it helpful to move with this exercise, so everything is kept free and open. The focus is on carving out the space in the mouth for the vowels.

○ When you have completed the monologue in vowels only, find natural alignment, let the breath settle, and speak the full monologue. Be aware of what has happened to the vowels as a result of the exercise.

Teacher tip

I use the mouthing, vowel dance and diphthong physicalizing for every monologue or scene as part of the early exploration that unlocks the language before we go on to the nuts and bolts of acting – objectives, tactics, blocking, etc. When language is in the body, the acting becomes more connected and clear.

Switching tongues

○ Create your own tongue-twister based on your first language to share with the rest of the class. If English is not your first language, you can have fun teaching a bit of your language to the rest of the class. If English is your first language, be creative and write phrases that exercise all your articulators, both consonants and vowels. Teach them to the class.

Teacher tip

In order to celebrate diversity and to give your English as a Second Language students an opportunity to "be the experts" you might have each student bring in a tongue-twister that they have created based in their first language and teach it to the class. This can be part of just one warm-up or become a regular part of your warm-up.

Colin's blog

We began by simply mouthing our sonnets to wake up and warm up our articulators. Then we did the vowels-only exercise. I felt a huge change in the amount of space in my mouth. It was fabulous. I am going to use this in my personal warm-up after I warm up the jaw and tongue to maximize space.

Kristina's blog

One thing we did today to arouse our articulators was mouthing. By having our concentration on our lips as we formed each part of every word, the words

were crisp and clean. The vowel dance was interesting. The vowels not only go to different places in my mouth, but I could feel them taking me to different places in my body too. I was fascinated by the diphthong exercise – to feel the sound start in one place in the mouth and move to another – because it is the marriage of two vowel sounds. With all the consonants, vowels and diphthongs, it felt like we were creating a savoury stew of speech sounds!

Discussion questions

What did you discover about vowels? In what ways does the "Vowels only" exercise change how and where you experience vowels in the mouth and in the body? What do vowels do for your emotional connection to the words? Discuss the specificity of long vowels in contrast with short vowels.

Teacher tip

What is included in this chapter barely scratches the surface of speech work. I would encourage you to go further with a couple of detailed resources. Louis Colaianni's excellent book The Joy of Phonetics *uses a unique approach to teaching the International Phonetic Alphabet (IPA) through phonetic-shaped pillows. It is very helpful for actors in really exploring the specificity of sound and giving them flexibility as they take on dialect work. Also, Dudley Knight's book,* Speaking with Skill (*to be published by Methuen Drama, April 2012), is an excellent creative and practical approach to the study of speech work.*

A word about dialects. I know there are many times when the plays you work on require specific dialects. I am also aware that young actors love to perform in dialect. I have some recommendations to help you and your students get to the best resources for creating authentic, believable and clear dialects.

I would first direct you to your new favorite website: International Dialects of English Archive (IDEA). This is the largest source of authentic dialects you are likely to find. The creator of the archives, Paul Meier, and his team of associate editors have scoured the world to find either ESL speakers or those who speak English with a regional dialect. Each speaker contributes a reading of a passage and personal stories about their lives so you can hear the nuances of their speech.

From a sample of an authentic individual dialect on the IDEA website, go to a dialect breakdown book for the specific signature sounds, stress, rhythm, intonation and practice sentences. I use Accents and Dialects for the Stage and Screen *by Paul Meier. He has accurate dialect breakdowns and excellent accompanying CDs for twenty-four dialects. His website is www.paulmeier.com.*

Another valuable dialect tool is The Dialect Handbook *by Ginny Kopf, which outlines the process for dialect acquisition: see www.voiceandspeechtraining.com. These two books together can help you create a whole curriculum for teaching dialects.*

With a sample of a real person to base your dialect on, an accurate breakdown of signature sounds and a CD, you and your actors will be well on your way to the creation of a clear and believable dialect.

Reflective voice blog

Now that you have learned about consonants and vowels, how they are defined and how they are formed, describe the ways in which your understanding and awareness of the specificity of sound have deepened. What exercises were the most effective for you? What will you take on as part of your personal practice?

Chapter 9 references

For more information on the topics discussed in this chapter refer to:

Barton, Robert, and Dal Vera, Rocco, *Voice Onstage and Off*, 2nd edn. New York and Oxford: Routledge, 2011.

Carey, David, and Clark Carey, Rebecca, *Vocal Arts Workbook and DVD*. London: Methuen Drama, 2008.

Colaianni, Louis, *The Joy of Phonetics and Accents*. New York: Drama Book Publishers, 1994.

Cook, Rena, "A Week with Andrew Wade", *Shakespeare Around the Globe*. Voice and Speech Review, 2005.

Espinosa, Micha, "A Call to Action: Embracing the Cultural Voice or Taming the Wild Tongue", *A World of Voice*. Voice and Speech Review, 2011.

Kopf, Ginny, *The Dialect Handbook*, Orlando: Voiceprint Publishing, 1997.

Meier, Paul, *Accents and Dialects for the Stage and Screen*. Lawrence: Paul Meier Dialect Service, 2009.

Parkin, Ken, *Anthology of British Tongue-Twisters*. London: Samuel French, 1969.

Rodenburg, Patsy, *The Actor Speaks*. London: Methuen Drama, 1997.

10 My personal warm-up

By now you have learned that the body and voice exercises you do are crucial, because they make your instrument ready to do the work. You are physically and vocally open, your muscles have been loosened, your focus sharpened. You are ready to bring your entire being to the work. The reality of the life of an actor is that you won't always have a teacher or director to guide you through a group warm-up – often you have to do it yourself. It is time now to create your own vocal warm-up. Out of all the exercises you have been exposed to, which ones really worked for you? Choose a sequence, and write it out in the space below. Be sure to include releasing and relaxing, alignment, deep breathing (including abdominal release), recoil breath, the moment of readiness, opening the vocal tract, stimulating vibrations and resonance, articulation, and working the body and voice together. This will give you the best possible warm-up of your entire instrument. As you choose your exercises, be mindful of the sequence; the order in which you do these exercises is important as well. Don't start with your biggest or highest sounds. Be gentle with your body and voice. Bring it to life slowly and methodically. A marathon runner doesn't start out sprinting; if she does, she will be hurt. So it is with actors and their voices. Take care of the voice, and it will last for ever.

My personal warm-up

Kristina's blog

Creating a personal warm-up forced me to evaluate my voice and focus on what warm-ups benefit me. I realized, after my warm-up, that I needed to incorporate more vocalization next time. I think that my personal warm-up just might need to be a little longer than most people's, because it usually takes me a little longer to release all my tension. I absolutely love this.

Colin's blog

We started the class with our personal warm-ups that we each brought to class. I really enjoyed warming up with my favorite exercises as well as observing what other people were doing. Some of the class did breath management, yoga, dowel rods, speaking sonnets with natural alignment, and connecting breath to thought. My warm-up consisted mainly of stretching, moving noise into all parts of the body, warming up my range, and finding optimum pitch. After the warm-up was complete, I felt great and just as warm and prepared for class as any time we did group warm-ups. This is a really great tool to gain because in auditions, rehearsals and performances, I want to be able to achieve this state of readiness so I am fully comfortable and tension-free.

Teacher tip

I assign the personal warm-up several days ahead of when it is due. The students all perform their individual warm-ups in class at the same time. They can use their notes. I watch and jot down general observations about the things I see them doing, mostly reinforcing the positives. I may also point out areas of concern; for example, if someone is doing an exercise that is vocally harmful or too aggressive too early, I will bring that to their attention. They then hand in their notes to me for final point assignments.

11 Expressivity: tennis balls and more

W e are now at a place in our vocal development where we need to start freeing up expressivity – releasing the voice to let it play. Expressivity is fully sounding the voice with all its qualities, rhythms, pitches, volume levels and emotional colors. It is about expanding comfort zones and pushing against vocal boundaries. What can my voice really do now that I understand how it works? I have aligned, I have breathed, I have vibrated, I have opened the vocal tract, I have expanded my range, and I have exercised my articulators. Now what?

This chapter features exercises that will help you find your free and released voice. It will help you bring together all the work you have done so far and help you discover how much your voice can actually do.

Teacher tip

Before the start of this exercise I explain a few simple guidelines: "Hold on to the tennis ball until I give you the directions. As we explore this exercise, you can't break anything in the room, and you can't hit another student with a tennis ball." If you have a large class, you can ask half the class to sit on the side and watch while you guide the first group through the entire exercise. Then switch out the groups. I give the seated group instructions to watch the progress of the exercise carefully to see and hear what shifts, changes or discoveries are made by the students. They will be asked to offer feedback at the conclusion of the exercise.

Tennis balls (DVD)

Each student will need a tennis ball for this exercise.

○ Without vocal sound, explore how many ways you can play with the tennis ball: throwing, tossing, rolling or bouncing. Be creative; if you explore one way and perfect that, find a new way. If someone else is doing something that is intriguing to you, try it. Have fun, be a five-year-old child again, and enjoy the opportunity to play imaginatively.

○ Continue playing with the tennis ball, and add open vowel sounds, letting the sound go wherever the tennis ball goes. If the ball goes up, the pitch goes up; if the ball goes down, the pitch goes down. The sound mirrors the movement of the tennis ball. Your voice is the sound of the tennis ball.

- Continue playing with the tennis ball and add text – any monologue – letting the words go where the ball goes. Be extravagant: don't worry about appropriate context or meaning, just let the words fly as the ball flies.

- Hold the tennis ball in your hand, feeling your feet grounded into the floor and length in the spine. Let the breath settle. Speak the text freely, allowing the monologue to be what it wants to be as a result of the tennis ball exploration.

Discussion questions

What did you notice about your voice through the sequence of this exploration? Did you notice anything happening with your pitch range? How did the vigorous physical exercise affect the voice? What aspects of the monologue were changed or made clearer?

⊙ Tennis ball with partner (DVD)

- Pair off, with one tennis ball for the two of you. Determine who is A and who is B.

- Partner A holds the tennis ball and leads partner B through the following sequence. B keeps his/her face twelve to fourteen inches from the ball at all times. A leads B up, down, side to side, or in circles with the tennis ball; B follows, sounding with open vowels. As in the exploration above, when the ball goes up, the pitch goes up. When the ball goes down, the pitch goes down. B should let the voice and body follow A's lead. A's job is to give B a vocal workout that encourages broad use of the voice, but does not endanger the voice or the body. You are partners, so work together.

- As A continues to lead the movement, B adds text, speaking the monologue freely, allowing the words to go where the ball goes.

- A stops and holds the tennis ball, making eye-contact with B. Partner B allows the breath to settle, then speaks the monologue to A, allowing the monologue to be whatever it wants to be as a result of the exploration.

137

○ Partners switch, following the above sequence. B holds the tennis ball and leads the movement while partner A sounds.

Discussion questions

What did you notice about your partner's voice through the sequence? What did you feel or observe in your own sound? How was the monologue different from previously?

Teacher tip

This exercise is great for dialogue work as well. In partners, each person can hold a ball. The character not speaking moves the ball for the character who is speaking, and they switch back and forth throughout the scene. The movement is abstract and not necessarily related to actual content of the scene. When the exploration is concluded, have them immediately do the scene within the context of the play. The result should be an energized connection between the actors and heightened clarity of language.

Five rhythms (DVD)

Many young actors fall into predictable rhythm, pitch, quality and volume patterns. Often they may perform a piece in exactly the same way as they first encountered it, settling into a deep pattern that is difficult to spark with new inspiration or stimulation. This type of delivery is seldom in the moment, spontaneous or connected to truth. When expanding expressivity, I look for explorations that shake up rote paths of delivery. The "Five rhythms", which has become a staple in my work with actors and text, is a sequence of exercises based on the work of dance researcher Gabrielle Roth, who defines all movement as falling into five rhythmic categories: *flow, staccato, chaos, lyric* and *stillness*. I have found that these rhythms are present in the voice as well. To explore these rhythms in the body and the voice, you will need music that stimulates the body to move freely. The best and most easily accessible is a CD by Gabrielle Roth herself, also a composer, called *Initiation*. The individual tracks are called "Flow", "Staccato", "Chaos", "Lyric" and "Stillness". You can, of course, use other music that has similar qualities. I have found both classical and contemporary rock music to be effective and fun as well.

Flow is movement that is about arches, curves and circles; it is grounded to the earth. It is about the gathering and releasing of body and breath – as the breath releases, the body opens; as breath is taken in, the body gathers toward its center. The music inspires this kind of movement. The vocal sounds that follow are also about flowing in arches, curves and circles.

Staccato is about short, angular movements which have beginnings, middles and ends. You can find staccato in all parts of the body. Staccato changes the breath. It affects the types of sounds the voice wants to make – short bursts of both vowels and consonants.

Chaos is loose, with no guidelines or restrictions. The words "rag doll" or "limp" may help when finding chaos. It does not always have to be done at energy-level ten, but it always accelerates the breath.

Lyric is the calm after the storm of chaos. It is floating, soaring, beyond the reach of gravity. Where flow is bound to the earth, lyric is flying above it. It is where the body and voice need to be after chaos. The breath begins to settle.

Stillness is about absence of physical movement, focusing on the movement of breath deep within the body. As you will see in the exercise below, some very powerful discoveries are made in stillness, when deep and genuine connections can be made that we miss in other rhythms because we are moving too fast to find them.

Teacher tip

The students will need one minute of memorized text for this sequence. I usually have them work with a legend or fairy tale. These types of stories are useful in expanding expressivity because they require a larger range of vocal commitment. This exercise can be taught over five class periods, with each rhythm taking a whole class (see the end of the chapter for alternative music selections). The entire sequence can also be taught in a single class period or, once taught, can be used as a fifteen-minute warm-up. You might find that you need to model the kinds of movement and sound to help the students get an accurate vision of what is required for this exercise. Once they get it, they will totally embrace it as a valuable tool that offers interpretative options they may never have thought of or discovered on their own. Discussion questions can come at the end of each rhythm or can be deferred until the entire exploration is completed.

○ **Flow** is full-body movement that is inspired by circles, arches and curves, and grounded to the earth.

○ Begin moving to the music (track 1 of *Initiation*), noticing the movement of the breath by exhaling on an easy *fff* sound. Enjoy releasing the body to the music and moving through space, exploring circles, arches and curves at various spacial levels of high, medium and low. Do this for several minutes.

○ Continue the flow movement and add open vowel sounds, letting the sound go where the body goes. Let pitches swoop and glide as the body swoops and glides. Accompany your movements with your own sound. Continue for several minutes.

○ Continuing the flow movement, add your text (monologue or legend), letting the words go as the body goes, in large and free curves, arches and circles. Continue for several minutes.

○ Stop the music, find your natural alignment, and let the breath settle. Speak your text, and allow the exploration you did with flow to influence the delivery of the thoughts.

○ **Staccato** is the opposite of flow; it is percussive, geometric, angular and punctuated. Start the music (track 2 of *Initiation*). Let the music inspire a new way of moving and a new breath pattern. Explore staccato in all parts of the body, not just arms. Try it in isolated parts of the body – a knee, a finger – then return to full-body exploration. Continue for several minutes.

○ Add sound. What does staccato sound like? Use vowels and consonants; use a variety of pitches and volume levels. Staccato does not have to be punching at energy-level ten. Continue for one minute.

○ Staying with the movement, add your text (monologue or legend), letting the words find the staccato rhythm. Don't worry that the rhythm does not fit the context. Continue for one minute.

○ Stop the music, find your natural alignment, and let the breath settle. Speak your text, and allow the exploration you did with staccato to influence the delivery of the thoughts. You may only find a couple of places where staccato really seems to fit, adding emphasis or stress to key phrases.

○ **Chaos** is full-body engagement – loose, limp, rag doll, no structure. It does *not* have to be full-out energy at level ten at all times, although it can, if that's what you feel compelled to do. Begin moving to the music (track 3 of *Initiation*) in whatever way it inspires you. Notice how the breath changes as you tax your body a bit more than you have done previously. Feel free, extravagant and robust. Continue for at least one minute.

○ Stop the music, and immediately speak your text from whatever is going on in your centre. Focus on a spot across the room and deliver the energy and thoughts toward that focal point.

○ **Lyric** is the calm after the storm: floating, flying and soaring beyond the reach of gravity. Begin moving to the music (track 4 of *Initiation*), and allow the body to move as the quality of the music inspires you. Notice the shifting quality of the breath, exhaling on an easy *shh* sound as you float and soar through the space. Continue for several minutes.

○ What does lyric sound like? Add the voice with open, free vowels. They may feel higher and lighter. Explore the upper pitches of the voice as you move through the space. Continue for several minutes.

○ Staying with the movement, add your text (monologue or legend), letting the words reflect the lyrical rhythm. Continue for several minutes.

○ Stop the music, find your natural alignment, and let the breath settle. Speak your text, and allow the exploration you did with lyric to influence the delivery of the thoughts.

○ **Stillness** is really about the lack of movement in the body and an awareness of the movement of the breath. To heighten that focus, move across the room as slowly as you can. You might imagine that you are running or swimming in slow motion. Start the music (track 5 of *Initiation*). Use an easy *shh* to mark the long exhales that live in stillness. Continue for two minutes.

○ Staying with stillness and the slow-motion movements, add open vowel sounds. Continue for two minutes.

○ Add text as you continue to explore slow-motion movement. Continue for several minutes.

○ Stop the music and the movement. Speak the text, allowing your inner sense of stillness to inform the thoughts.

○ Now that you have experienced each rhythm separately and know the qualities that each can draw from the text, do your own fully physicalized and vocalized exploration of all five within your own monologue or legend. Change from rhythm to rhythm randomly – don't let your intellect take over. They don't even have to be in order. Some rhythms may seem to suit the text perfectly; others may not. That is OK at this point.

○ When you have explored your monologue, ground yourself, find natural alignment, and let the breath truly settle. Speak your text, allowing the rhythms to inform both your speech and your body.

Teacher tip

You can have the students do their final full five-rhythms exploration for a partner. First one performs, the other witnesses and then offers feedback at the end; then they switch. I have also done this as a performance assignment. The entire class sits in a circle on the floor and watches as each student does a full-out five-rhythms exploration, then shifts into speaking the piece. I evaluate on the integration of body and voice, the effective and spontaneous use of the rhythms, and how much the voice was brought out in terms of pitch range, inflection patterns, volume variety, quality variety and rhythmic variety. Things to watch for usually revolve around body engagement that overpowers the voice, letting the voice go into dangerous places where students could be hurting themselves (this doesn't often happen when body is moving freely), or movement unconnected to the voice. I come back to this exercise many times in both class and rehearsal settings.

Discussion questions

How did the "Five rhythms" change your legend? Which rhythm worked best for you? Why? Which one surprised you? Why? What happened to your pitch range through this sequence of exercises? What vocal quality changes did you observe? How might this tool be used for other monologues or scenes?

Here is a list of additional music that has been effective for this exercise:

Flow

Romeo and Juliet, movie soundtrack, track 3
Mascani, *Cavalleria Rusticana*, "Intermezzo"
Mozart, *Piano Concerto No. 21 in C*, "Elvira Madigan"
Virgin, *Chillout Mix*, Craig Armstrong, "Balcony Scene Romeo and Juliet"
Geoffrey Oryema, *Beat the Border*, "Lapwony"

Staccato

Romeo and Juliet, movie soundtrack, track 1 or 8
Moby, *Play*, "Run On", track 11
Saint-Saens, *Symphony No. 3 in C Minor*, "Organ"
Geoffrey Oryema, *Beat the Border*, "The River"
Vivaldi, *Four Seasons*, 1st Movement

Chaos

Moby, *Play*, "Machete", track 8
Iggy Pop, *Lust for Life*, "Some Weird Sin"

Geoffrey Oryema, *Beat the Border*, "Lajok"
Romeo and Juliet, movie soundtrack, track 10
Handel, *Messiah*, "Hallelujah Chorus"

Lyric

Beethoven, *Symphony No. 6 in F*, "Pastoral"
Vaughan Williams, "The Lark Ascending"
Romeo and Juliet, movie soundtrack, track 13
Elgar, *Variations on an Original Theme*, "Enigma"

Stillness

Beethoven, *Moonlight Sonata*, Sonata in C Sharp Minor
Barber, "Adagio for Strings"
Fauré, *Requiem*, "In Paradisum"
Moby, *Play*, "Down Slow", track 12
Allegri, "Miserere"

Colin's blog

*We finished class by reciting our legends in all five rhythms.
This brought new life to my legend, and I loved the sense of
variety that I discovered while doing it. Between flow,
staccato, chaos, lyric and stillness, lyric is definitely my
favorite. It is similar to flow except flow is more grounded.
Lyric is supposed to be like sailing, flying above and on top of
things. This is my type of movement and rhythm. When I find
something that helps me access the space above my head
I get excited. I feel it is important to connect with one of the
rhythms and then branch out from there so that each rhythm
takes on its own characteristics and traits within you.*

Kristina's blog

*I really like the transition from lyric to stillness because they
are the exact opposite of each other – they are so totally
different. It was great to go from an elevated and energetic
state to one that is low and intense. I am interested in playing
opposites, like when a character is one way on the outside,
while something really different is happening on the inside.
That is what stillness feels like for me. So little is happening
on the outside, but so much is churning inside.*

143

Reflective voice blog

Take some time to put down in words how the tennis-ball exploration and the "Five rhythms" influenced your monologue or legend. What new things did you discover about the text in regard to interpretation and vocal variety? What parts of this will you take on as part of your regular personal practice?

In my first language

○ Try speaking your monologue first in your native language. Don't worry if it does not translate exactly; speak the essence in the language closest to your heart; speak with conviction, own the thoughts, even if the words are not exact.

○ Now speak the monologue in English.

Teacher tip

For many of our students, English is not their first language. Having to act in English can be frustrating for them, making them feel self-conscious and not as good as others in the class. It is difficult to free the voice when the actor has first to translate thoughts into their native tongue in order to have true understanding and emotional connection to the meaning. In the past decade, the voice and acting field has begun to acknowledge this issue and research strategies for serving these students with celebration of their diversity. I have tried allowing ESL students to deliver their monologues in their native language, to take the essence of the speech and improvise it ("What would this sound like in your language?"), or as homework, to translate it into their language and perform it for the class. If speaking in their native language gives them access to a freer, more connected voice, then victory! I have included some of these performances in final showings or recitals.

Cultural voice

Bring in one minute of text that you have found in a play, a poem, a song, or something you have written that is based on or reflects your culture of origin. This is a celebration of your roots, your heritage. It can reflect your own family's values, a holiday tradition, a cultural event, national pride or triumph over adversity (either personal or cultural).

Teacher tip

To celebrate the diversity and cultural heritage of your students, "Cultural voice" can be adapted to suit the specific make-up of your class. I have also done a version of this under the title of "Heritage project". It can be a whole unit where you work on their selections in class by following the "monologue sequence" (as outlined in Chapter 12) over several class periods. This could culminate in a final showing as the students add movement, costume or music.

Political speech

This is an excellent exercise to explore power without press or push by using a two-minute excerpt from a political speech that inspires you. To find one, go to www.americanrhetoric. com/top100speechesall.html or www.historyplace.com/speeches, where you will find "The Great Speech Collection", with written transcriptions of famous speeches. The goal of this assignment is not to imitate the person who originally spoke these words, but to find the inspiration within yourself to make these great words your own. How would these words sound if you spoke them? What in your world would inspire you with the need to express these thoughts?

○ With a copy of your speech in hand, find natural alignment, connect to a deep breath, and begin speaking, breathing at each thought-shift. Resist the temptation to act or be inspiring; just connect breath to thought.

○ Read again, still breathing at thought-shifts. Add more space in the mouth. Feel space in the throat and in your center. Resist the desire to act or press for power.

○ At volume-level two or three, speak each part of every word, fully wrapping your mouth around each syllable.

○ With a pencil, circle each noun that is clearly a person, place or thing. Read it again, making space in the mouth for each word. This time physicalize each noun as you speak it.

○ Circle the verbs, particularly the verbs that indicate action of some kind. Find natural alignment, connect to a deep breath, and speak the speech again, this time physicalizing each verb.

○ Reconnect with natural alignment and deep central breathing. Read the entire two-minute cutting, allowing the work you did on nouns and verbs easily to inform the reading. *Let* it happen; resist *making* it happen. Just see if the speech has a little more clarity and forward momentum.

Teacher tip

The next sequence of exercises is led or coached by you, working with individual students with the rest of class assisting in the various explorations. I usually have the class seated in a circle on the floor. The speaker stands, finds natural alignment, connects to breath, and just speaks the speech to provide a starting point. I encourage the speaker to work authentically, not manufacturing power through pressing or imitating the original speaker. All the subsequent explorations are intended to help the actor find authentic power, expressivity, as well as clarity and specificity of images.

For the next sequence, you will need to have the speech memorized.

○ Three students stand behind the speaker, offering support; another group of students face the speaker as if they are the intended audience. Feel the presence of your support team; breathe in the power and confidence that they provide. When you feel grounded and centered, begin the speech.

○ To the three supporting students: when the speaker makes a strong point, or you feel compelled to communicate support, place a hand on the speaker's shoulder.

○ Audience members can also offer support by applauding or standing in agreement when they are inspired to do so.

Discussion questions

How did the presence of support affect the speaker? What moments felt strong and authentic?

○ Members of the class are now going to offer some resistance. They do not agree. It is the speaker's job to overcome their objections. The audience can express disagreement on specific points by turning away or even verbally disagreeing. The speaker may move among the resistance, speaking to individuals to win support.

Discussion questions

How did the presence of resistance affect the speech? What moments or responses felt authentic and powerful? How does it feel to try to overcome objections? What verbal and physical tools did you discover?

Teacher tip

I don't let the resistance get so strong that it verbally overpowers the speaker. If the speaker begins to work too hard vocally, I encourage her to reconnect with her center and find the strength lower and deeper. You can also control help from the class by saying they can start with resistance, but the speaker wins them over so that they all end up in agreement.

Peopling the speech

Speeches become clearer as the speaker really sees what they are talking about. This exploration helps the actor find specificity of imagery.

○ As famous speeches often refer to or describe individuals or groups, count how many such references are mentioned in your speech. If there are, say, four, have four students stand at various places in the circle. Give them their assignments – for example, "You are the starving children and you are the poverty-stricken mothers." As you say your speech, each time you refer to the children or the mothers walk toward or motion to that student. Instead of just saying the phrase, you have to find them and really see them as you speak about them.

Teacher tip

The scenario for peopling the speech must change from speaker to speaker according to the needs of the particular speech. Be inventive; create explorations that will help the students discover the images they are speaking of. If the text speaks of events more than people, have students represent the events. For example, "Each time you talk about that battle, look at or walk toward this group. Make your audience see what you see. Make them feel about this person or event the way you feel about it." If, as another example, the speech is about an historic battle, have the class be the soldiers who fought in the battle. Have the speaker walk among them, addressing each separately or placing a hand on their shoulder. The idea is to help the student find specificity and personalize the piece. You might also consider some guided imagery to help them personalize the given circumstances out of which the speech was originally created. A final performance can be the culminating activity of your work with political speeches. It can be useful to let the student set up the exploration that he/she found most helpful and perform the speech as an outgrowth of the exploration. This helps to subvert the desire to go back into "performance mode".

Reflective voice blog

What did you learn from the political speech assignment? What part of the exercise made you feel the most connected and powerful? What is the difference for you between authentic power and pressing for power? What did you learn about the importance of specificity?

Chapter 11 references

For more information on the topics discussed in this chapter refer to:

Berry, Cecily, *The Actor and the Text*. Montclair: Applause Theatre Books, 2000.

Boston, Jane, and Cook, Rena, eds, *Breath in Action: The Art of Breath in Vocal and Holistic Practice*. London: Jessica Kinsley Publishers, 2009.

Carey, David, and Clark Carey, Rebecca, *Verbal Arts Workbook*. London: Methuen Drama, 2010.

Cook, Rena, "A Week with Andrew Wade", *Shakespeare Around the Globe, Voice and Speech Review*, 2005.

Espinosa, Micha, "A Call to Action: Embracing the Cultural Voice or Taming the Wild Tongue", *A World of Voice, Voice and Speech Review, 2011*.

Gronbeck-Tedesco, John, *Acting Through Exercises*. Mountain View: Mayfield Publishing Company, 1992.

Rodenburg, Patsy, *Speaking Shakespeare*. New York: Palgrave Macmillan, 2002.

Roth, Gabrielle, *Maps to Ecstasy: A Healing Journey for the Untamed Spirit*. Novato: New World Library, 1998.

Exercises

The "Five Rhythms" exercise was adapted from the work of Gabrielle Roth by Debbie Green and Morwenna Rowe, Central School of Speech and Drama. The "Political Speech" sequence was adapted from work created by David Carey.

12

Perfect voice!
Now what?

In the end, it all comes down to the acting, doesn't it? If you are a drama student, and you want to be cast in a show, you have to act the role with vocal clarity, physical specificity and authenticity. When I am casting, the one thing that I look for first is honesty. Do I believe them? Can this actor authentically convey the inner world of the character? So now that you have a deeper understanding of how to use your voice, let's look at how you can use the voice in the service of truth, developing what is real and authentic in the character and clearly sharing it with an audience.

Voice is connected to your center, breath is connected to your center, your emotions are connected to your center, and your needs, desires and objectives are connected to your center. Do you see a common thread emerging? It all comes back to connecting to your center. The truth is in your center, the truth is in the breath, the truth is in the body – it is not in your head. We can analyze, we can write character sketches, we can make up imaginary backgrounds, and we can dig into given circumstances – all these are valuable and important parts of the actor's standard homework. But if the work stops there, the truth will stop there as well – it will stay in your head. The work of this chapter is how to find the truth in acting – how to use the voice to access your personal truth so you can bring it fully and clearly to the stage.

Monologue sequence

Choose a monologue to work on for this sequence. It is more effective if you have the monologue memorized, but it can also be an effective way to work up a new monologue.

○ Find natural alignment. Connect to the natural rhythm of the breath. Focus on the moment when the inhale becomes the exhale. Once that is established, begin speaking the text, connecting breath to word and breathing at punctuation. Resist the temptation to "act". Simply connect breath to thought.

○ Repeat the above instructions, and add more space in the mouth.

○ Do the monologue with vowels only (see Chapter 7, pages 100–101). Move easily if that is helpful. Keep the breath flowing freely as you change from vowel to vowel, and avoid harsh glottal attacks.

○ Speak the monologue, relishing the space that has been carved out in the mouth by the vowel-only exercise.

○ Mouth the monologue, fully activating the lips, teeth and tongue.

- Come back to natural alignment and connect with the breath. Speak the monologue again, paying the same kind of attention to the lips, teeth and tongue that you did in the previous exercise.

- Speak the text and physicalize the last word of each sentence.

- Sing the monologue. Make up a tune; it can be opera, musical theatre, rock 'n' roll, upbeat, or a ballad. Whatever your choice, commit fully and just sing! If you feel the need to move as well, you can improvise choreography to go with your song.

Teacher tip

You can also use "Pitch absurd", "Master thespian", "Five rhythms" or "Tennis balls" here, or any combination thereof. The intention here is to shake up inflection patterns, get the voice into the body, and find physical and vocal ease.

- Now speak the monologue, allowing whatever you gained from the singing to influence you as it will.

- Take a moment now to imagine the given circumstances of the monologue. As you do this, close your eyes and breathe deeply. The given circumstances can be within the context of the play or they can be created out of your imagination. Consider such questions as: "Where am I?" "How do I feel about where I am?" "Who am I with?" "How do I feel about who I am with?" See the answers to these questions specifically and clearly in your mind's eye. Breathe these images into your center. What do I want? How badly do I want it? Where in my body do I feel the need? Be clear, be specific, and breathe your images into your center. It is not enough to know them in your mind; know them in your body as well. Picture the person you are speaking to. See a specific face. For the sake of this exercise it helps to picture a person you know very well and for whom you have strong feelings. Place that face and what you need to do to or get from that person in your center, and connect it to the breath. Open your eyes, see the face, and speak to that person. Trust the power of the breath to carry your words to the "other".

Discussion questions

How did the monologue change through the sequence of these exercises? What discoveries did you make about your monologue? What did you learn about your character? What happened to your emotional connection? Where did you feel the connection in the body? What did you notice about language? How did the voice change from the beginning of the exercise to the end?

Reflective voice blog

Using those discussion questions to guide your thoughts, reflect on what you learned from the monologue sequence above.

⊙ Fun with monologues (DVD)

Sometimes the truth of a monologue can be found by turning the monologue on its head, so to speak.

- Randomly pick two characters and accompanying scenarios that bear no similarities to the character of the monologue. For example, if you are doing a Juliet monologue, pick a five-year-old child who is caught with his hand in the cookie jar and a demanding teacher punishing an unruly child.

- Perform the monologue first as the child caught in the act. Really commit and go all out with your choice.

- Then perform the monologue as the punishing teacher, with full commitment.

- Then perform Juliet again within the real given circumstances.

Teacher tip

To kick start the students' creativity, I sometimes ask for character and scenario suggestions from the class and list ten or twelve of each on the board. Sometimes this is assigned as homework to give them time to create and rehearse, but sometimes it is totally improvised. Either way is effective.

Discussion questions

What discoveries did you make about your monologue? How did it change from other run-throughs? What did the two imaginary characters do for the real character? In what ways was the monologue deepened?

Colin's blog

The thing I really loved about "Fun with monologues" is that I found myself not even thinking about the words; they simply came to me naturally and truthfully. I felt so focused, yet at times so free. Kristina's two characters were a little girl getting paddled and a sad woman at a funeral. When she performed her monologue naturally, her optimum pitch was easily discovered, she had perfect diction, and her breath support was right with her.

Reflective voice blog

Take a few minutes to reflect on what you gained from "Fun with monologues". Look not only at what choices you made and how they informed the monologue, but also at what you saw in others. How did this assignment affect your fellow classmates? What can you learn from their lessons?

⊙ Two chairs (DVD)

The purpose of this exercise is to clarify transitions and track the journey of the character's thoughts. It can be done one at a time with the class observing, or it can be done by the entire class working in pairs.

○ Place two armless chairs side by side. The speaker sits in one chair while the partner sits on the floor facing the speaker. Throughout, the speaker addresses the seated partner, making solid eye-contact. If still on book, eye-contact is made whenever possible.

○ The speaker begins. At the first thought-change, the speaker moves to the other chair. At each thought-change, the speaker moves back and forth from one chair to the other. Care is taken that the movement itself happens in silence; the next thought cannot begin until the speaker is firmly planted in the new chair.

○ At the conclusion of the monologue, the partner on the floor gives feedback on what they noticed was happening to the monologue and what parts stood out or were clearer.

○ Partners switch positions and repeat the same sequence.

Teacher tip

A single demonstration is helpful to give the class an understanding of what the exercise looks like. Usually time does not allow each speaker to work this exercise in front of the class. After each partner has had an opportunity to change chairs, then the class as a whole can discuss what was observed. By asking "What did you notice in your partner's work?" good responses begin to flow.

Discussion questions

What was clarified as you worked through this exercise? What did you learn about the journey of the character's thoughts? What was made clearer about the rhythm of breathing patterns?

Operative words

Operative words are key words – the nouns and verbs of your monologue. Young actors often don't take the time to visualize fully what they are speaking about. All words are not equal; some demand more time, more thought and more energy in performance. Nouns and verbs carry meaning; they are crucial in conveying actual content to an audience. What is this speech really about? What are the two or three words in each sentence that the audience must hear in order to know what is going on?

○ Underline the nouns in your monologue. Those words that convey a person, place, thing or animal.

○ Read the monologue and physicalize each noun. Do a movement that is large and full-body − it does not have to be literal. Relish the nouns − give them time and color and bring them to life with your entire body.

○ Find natural alignment and breathe. Speak the monologue, retaining what you learned about the nouns.

○ Underline the action verbs.

○ Read the monologue and physicalize each verb. Find the action in your entire body. You may be inspired to be literal − perhaps you run if the verb is "run" − but you can also be more abstract. The point is to activate each verb by putting it in your body.

○ Find natural alignment and breathe. Speak the monologue, retaining what you learned about the verbs.

Discussion questions
How did the monologue change? What did you learn about nouns and verbs?

Working with duets
The same concepts of taking voice work into acting can be done with scene work as well.

Teacher tip
Even if the actors are still on book, they can do this exercise. Have them look down at the page, get the line in their mind, look up, make eye-contact, and speak the line to their partner. This pattern is repeated throughout the exercise: read the line, then look up and say it, making eye-contact.

○ Choose a duet. Face your partner, either sitting or standing. Focus first on connecting to the breath, breathing together; establish a natural breathing rhythm together. Just speak each line making eye-contact with your partner. Resist the temptation to act; just connect breath to thought.

- Repeat the instructions as stated above, but this time also *reaching* your partner with your words. Imagine that the breath is carrying the words all the way to the partner. Make space in your mouth so that the words have the energy to reach your partner.

- Repeat the scene, still making eye-contact and breathing. This time, allow your words to *affect* your partner. Conversely, on each inhale, allow yourself to be affected by what you hear.

- Repeat the scene. This time take your partner's hands and squeeze gently on the words you want to stress.

- Sit on the floor back to back, with backs touching. Repeat the scene, gently pressing against the back of your partner on words you want to stress. Since you are not facing your partner, the breath will need to power the words a little more so your partner can still hear you.

- Now stand and face your partner, staying at a distance of four to five feet. Staying with the breath and maintaining eye-contact, *reach* and *affect* your partner from this distance with the power of the words. Allow yourself to be affected by your partner as well.

- If you now need to integrate the scene into the rest of a rehearsal, play the scene within the context of the blocking, maintaining the sense of connection and the need to affect with your words.

Play catch

- As you are repeating the scene, play a game of catch. Easily toss a ball back and forth, and let the game inform how you speak the scene. It can be playful, competitive, serious, casual or intimate. Allow the game to reflect what is going on in the scene.

- If you want to raise the stakes, a game of keep-away can help. The person who wants control struggles to get the ball from the other who is withholding it.

Tug-of-war

- Stretch a long rope or a long piece of fabric between you. Speak the dialogue. The rope is the energy connection between the two of you. Don't ever let it go totally slack. You can swing the rope, you can wrap it round each other, you can tug on it, you can tease with it, or you can threaten with it. Let the rope be the reflection of what you want from your partner. Don't plan, but let this be spontaneous play and see what discoveries you make.

> **Teacher tip**
> *These duet exercises can be done early in the process as part of table work. They can also be used in work rehearsals. If a scene has gone stale, or the stakes are low, or language is not clear, you can use one of these exercises. Then have them go immediately back into the actual blocking and see what carries over from the exploration.*

King of the mountain

Often within a duet or multi-character scene, power shifts back and forth. At one moment character A may have the upper hand, but then it can shift so that character B emerges as dominant. These shifts in scenes are subtle and sometimes hard to detect, but they are none the less absolutely essential to the overall performance. "King of the mountain" can be used to help you find the natural ebb and flow of dominance within a duet or scene.

You will need a small object that can be stood on, such as a yoga mat, a short cube or stool, even a circle drawn on the floor. This is the "mountain".

○ Begin speaking the scene. When it feels that your character has the upper hand or is fighting for dominance, move to the top of the mountain. If it feels that your character has lost the upper hand, move off. You can also remove someone from the mountain if you want to claim the spot. Right or wrong doesn't matter at this point. If you have the slightest inkling that your character may be gaining in status, take your place on the mountain.

Discussion questions

What did you learn about the ebb and flow of status in your scene? How many times did it shift? Does one character seem to have status more than another? How did it feel to claim status? How did it feel to be deposed? What changes in your voice or use of language occurred at the points of transition?

Words as darts

This is a good duet exercise which infuses energy and focus into the words; it conveys the idea that each word can be used as a tactic to get at your partner. The goal for each player is to use your own words as darts to land on the partner, while alternately shielding yourself from your partner's words. Each player finds an object that can be used as a shield – a piece of cardboard, a box, a pillow or a chair – which they carry with them.

○ Begin the scene. The first speaker uses every word as if it were a dart, following the other actor around the space, spitting words as if they were weapons. The other shields himself and attempts to dodge out of the way of the flying words.

○ As the speaker shifts, the actors alternate between landing their own words or shielding themselves from their partner's words, always moving freely through the space. This is a high-energy exercise full of movement and sound.

Teacher tip

I find myself side-coaching pretty actively through this exercise. "Use your words, your words are darts, make them land." "Protect yourself, use that shield, get away from those flying darts." "Every word is a dart."

When "Words as darts" has run its course, go immediately back into the context of the play and perform the scene, allowing the energy and clarity of the exercise to inform the scene.

Where in your body?

I have said that it is not enough to have a mental understanding of a character, a moment, a need or an objective. You must also know it in your body. The body's memory for emotions, images, trauma, joy or desire is profound. It is deeper, more honest and more specific than memory carried solely in the brain or the mind. Body knowledge is also more useful to the actor. Granted it can be more difficult to access, but it is the sure path to authentic, truthful and transformative acting. For most performers, the first repository for artistic choices is the intellect. It takes some work for us to dig deeper. You may have already been told by directors or acting teachers, "You're in your head – get out of your head and into your body." The question is always, "How do I do that?" The following series of exercises is designed to wake up the body's memory, making it a more useful and immediate source for an actor's truth.

If I were to ask you, "Where in your body do you feel love?" you would be able to touch the specific part where you most actively feel love. Do you feel jealousy in a different place? When you are angry, what part of your body is most alive? My guess is that your body knows exactly where it feels specific emotions. Now let me ask you a slightly different question: "Where in your body do you most vividly recall your mother?" Let's assume for the sake of this discussion that you have an annoying little brother. "Where in your body do you feel the memory of his latest antic?" Now, if you tell me a story of your little brother with an awareness of where in your body you are remembering him, will it look and sound different than if you are telling me a story about your mother with an awareness of where in your body you remember her? The answer is: of course. This would happen without your even thinking about it. Your voice and body would change because of your deep and specific body memory; you know these two people because they are truly part of your entire memory system – mind and body.

Now let's take this discussion to a character you are playing. Characters don't have the same depth of physical memory unless we give it to them. Characters have words to say that reveal who they are, how they feel and what they want. However, unless we push their memory, images, feelings and desires into our bodies, their words are likely to remain in our head, superficial and artificial. We must ask our characters these same questions: "Where in the body do you feel that?" "Where in the body do you see her?" "Where in your body do you recognize that need?"

The exercise I call "Where in your body" repeatedly asks the questions, "Where in your body do you feel that need?" "Where in your body do you feel the memory of him?" "Where in your body do you see that image?" It is either coached by a teacher or by a partner.

- Partner A, feel your feet against the floor, find natural alignment; connect to the breath by focusing on the moment the inhale becomes the exhale. Begin speaking the monologue.

- Partner B, stand across from your partner by several feet. Listen carefully to the monologue. Listen for the mention of a person, an image, a place or a need. Simply and quietly ask, "Where in your body do you see, hear, remember . . . " etc.

- Partner A, without giving it too much thought, point to the place on your body where you feel that person or image. There is no right or wrong; don't second-guess yourself, just point.

- Slowly work through the monologue. In a one-minute monologue, there may be four questions with four different places in the body identified.

- Repeat the monologue straight through and touch the parts of the body identified in the previous work-through.

- Repeat the monologue without specifically touching the body, but maintain an awareness of where in the body the memories were centered.

Discussion questions

What changes in levels did you notice in yourself or in your partner as you worked through this exercise? What new discoveries did you notice? What aspects of the monologue were deepened?

Teacher tip

This is deep and challenging work, but the results are so worth the effort. It will take some modeling from you before the students are able to identify the moments that can be remembered in the body. Even if you start with one or two per monologue, you are making headway. Acting deepens as the choices are rooted more firmly in the body. The instinct to press in order to manufacture feelings or needs diminishes as the power of body memory replaces it. Acting is less effortful, but it holds more power and believability.

Reflective voice blog

How has your understanding of voice and acting deepened through this chapter? Which of the exercises helped you deepen your work and how? What shifted in your work through the partner exercises in terms of relationship and connection?

Chapter 12 references

For more information on the topics discussed in this chapter refer to:

Barton, Robert, and Dal Vera, Rocco, *Voice Onstage and Off*, 2nd edn. New York and Oxford: Routledge, 2011.

Berry, Cecily, *The Actor and the Text*. Montclair: Applause Theatre Books, 2000.

Boston, Jane, and Cook, Rena, eds, *Breath in Action: The Art of Breath in Vocal and Holistic Practice*. London: Jessica Kinsley Publishers, 2009.

Carey, David, and Clark Carey, Rebecca, *Verbal Arts Workbook*. London: Methuen Drama, 2010.

Gronbeck-Tedesco, John, *Acting Through Exercises*. Mountain View: Mayfield Publishing Company, 1992.

Rodenburg, Patsy, *Speaking Shakespeare*. New York: Palgrave Macmillan, 2002.

Exercises

"Where in Your Body?" was adapted from an exercise shared with me by Rocco Dal Vera.

13 Sample warm-ups

Vocal warm-ups are crucial in the life of an actor. They are not just a part of training that can be learned once then set aside, as in, "Done that, check." Voice work should be done every day. Just as an athlete must work out daily to keep muscles strong and skills sure, so the actor must keep the vocal and physical instrument sharp, flexible and toned through daily warm-ups. This chapter offers several sample warm-ups of varying lengths that will start you on the road to building better and better vocal strength, control and clarity. I would encourage you to perform these with a great deal of focus and attention. Make every warm-up an opportunity to learn something new about your voice, to increase your awareness. Don't let yourself go on auto-pilot, going through the motions without true attention. Be mentally present whether you have thirty minutes or five.

Ideally, you will develop your own sequence of warm-up exercises that works for you. Each of us is different, and our bodies and voices respond better to certain exercises than to others. Some of the activities presented throughout this book will have worked well for you, and some may not have. Take on the ones that work, set aside those that don't. As you learned when you developed your personal warm-up in Chapter 10, there is a natural sequence to follow:

o Release and stretch the body.

o Find natural alignment.

o Get grounded and centered.

o Connect to a deep central breath including abdominal release and moment of readiness.

o Open the vocal tract.

o Wake up vibrations.

o Energize the articulators.

o Get the body and sound moving together.

o Connect words to an authentic need to speak.

Wake up the body and voice gently, gradually raising the effort level as you go.

⊚ Full warm-up (DVD)

Allow thirty minutes.

○ Yawn and stretch, arms reaching up and out, roll shoulders, shake legs, move face around.

○ Find your feet hip-width apart, toes pointed straight ahead, weight spread evenly on the balls of the feet and the heels.

○ Find softness in ankles and knees with a little bouncy "oingo, boingo".

○ Bring awareness to the pelvic girdle and hips, and feel length in the lower spine.

○ Sense your spine as it builds from the tailbone to your neck, starting with the lower back, moving through your middle back, and building through your upper back to your neck. Feel the head floating on top of your spine.

○ Feel the jaw hang loose, your tongue resting on the floor of the mouth.

○ Put a circle in your right ankle; add an easy hum as you move the ankle. Put a circle in your other ankle, adding an easy hum.

○ Put a large, sloppy circle in your hips. Add an easy "ah" in a comfortable part of your pitch range. Change directions. Feel the sound as the perfect accompaniment to the movement.

○ Swing your arms like a child, twisting easily from side to side.

○ Stretch the ribcage and intercostals by extending one arm up and over and "patting the pony". Make an easy "yummy" sound as you do this.

○ Roll your shoulders with an "ee".

○ Swing one arm like a windmill with an "oo". Then swing the other arm, also with an "oo".

○ Drop the head forward. Let the chin rest on the chest and shake the head, "no".

○ Slowly lift the head. As you look right, exhale on "shh". As you look left, inhale. Repeat slowly several times.

○ Let your chin drop to the chest and slowly roll down the spine. Release the head, shoulders and knees. Breathe deeply into your lower back, feeling the lower back lift slightly toward the ceiling on each inhale. Sigh out several sighs of relief. Shake out some sound.

- Slowly roll up, one vertebra at a time. The head is the last to come up.

- Walk across the dowel rods (Chapter 4).

- T'ai chi with dowel rod (Chapter 7).

- Check in with abdominal release (Chapter 6).

- Wake up the recoil breath (Chapter 6).

- Bring awareness to the moment of readiness (Chapter 6).

- Hum through to wake up vibrations (Chapter 7).

- The archer (Chapter 7).

- Open vocal tract: jaw, tongue, throat, soft palate (Chapter 7).

- Extend pitch range with "ng" siren (Chapter 8).

- Recall optimum pitch with the Pringles tube. Try a few lines of text using optimum pitch (Chapter 8).

- Wake up the articulators with "Consonant conga" or mouthing some text (Chapter 9).

- Dance or sing the text. You can also use part or all of the "Five rhythms". "Tennis ball" is also an option (Chapter 11).

- Ground and let the breath settle. Speak the text from wherever the last exploration left you.

- Connect back with natural alignment and deep central breath. Think of your character's central objective and breathe it into your center. When you are connected to the real need, speak the text.

Hum through

Humming through body parts is an efficient way to warm up if time is limited and the space you are in doesn't permit fully sounding.

- Put a hum in your ankles while circling each.

- Put a hum in your hips as you circle them.

- Put a hum in your waist as you swing from side to side.

- Put a hum in your shoulders as you roll them backward and forward.

Voice and the young actor

○ Put a hum in each arm as you swing it full circle.

○ Put a hum in your head as you look gently to the right and to the left.

○ Put a hum in your head as you circle it gently.

○ Put a hum in your face and move it around.

○ Chew a hum.

○ Hum through your pitch range from easy low notes, through your mid-range to easy upper notes.

○ Move a frothy hum through your whole body, moving the body easily with the sound.

Warm-up to build ensemble energy

○ Take a brisk walk around the room, observing everything in the space as if you have never seen it before. As you notice other people in the space, acknowledge them with an easy smile.

○ Stop and ground. Imagine you are taking a lovely warm shower. Rub your face, neck and arms as if to wash yourself clean.

○ Walk again. Give a high-five to each person you pass.

○ Stop and ground. Connect with the breath by putting a hand below your navel. Feel the movement out as the breath drops in. Feel the movement in as your breath leaves the body. Speak an energized "ha" on each exhale.

○ Walk again. Give a double high-five to each person you pass.

○ Stop and ground. Blow through your lips, humming on loops of pitch. Change to "oo" on loops of pitch. Change to "ee" on loops of pitch. Change to "vvv" on loops of pitch. Change to "zz" on loops of pitch.

○ Walk again. Hug each person you meet.

○ Stop and ground. Speak a monologue or sonnet softly, fully pronouncing every part of every word.

○ Walk again. When you come to another person, stop. Take them in with your eyes and your breath. One of you speaks a line of your sonnet or monologue. The other answers with a line from their sonnet or monologue.

○ Walk again. Find another person. Stop. Take them in with your eyes and your breath. One of you speaks a line of your sonnet or monologue. The other answers with a line from their sonnet or monologue.

○ Walk again. Find another person. Stop. Take them in with your eyes and your breath. Speak half of your sonnet or monologue with the objective to affect your partner with your words. The other answers with half of their sonnet or monologue, with the same objective.

Dance, observe, name moments

This is an excellent warm-up for energizing, focusing, sharpening observation and building an ensemble. It should be done to music that inspires energetic rhythmic dance, such as Miriam Makeba's *Welela*.

○ When the music starts, begin dancing and moving to the music. Keep your eyes up; your focus is on observing. Observe the space as if you have never seen it before and you want to memorize every detail. Move to the music and observe. Don't feel you have to "dance well", just move however your body wants to respond to the music.

○ Pick out specific objects or locations in the space and energize them with your focus and your movement. For example, you can "dance with the ceiling", and send your energy to the ceiling as you dance and observe. "Dance with a chair" and send and receive energy from the chair as you dance and observe. Form relationships with objects and places in the space with your movement, energy and focus. Feel the objects energize you. Do this for several minutes.

○ Add starting and stopping. At any point, stop the movement and stand completely still, feeling the total stillness. When you are ready, begin to move again from a specific point on your body – for example, a pulse in the top of your head starts the movement again. Dance and observe until you stop again, feel the stillness, and activate from a pulse in another part of your body. Start and stop for several minutes.

○ Add taking photos. Now when you stop, take a mental picture of what you see. So now you are dancing and observing, starting and stopping, and when you stop you are taking a mental photo. Do this for several minutes.

○ Add naming moments. This time when you stop and take your mental photo, name the picture out loud as if labeling a work of art. For example, when you stop, you might see a book bag on a chair. You say out loud, "Book bag on chair," let a pulse move you, and begin to dance again. Keep dancing, observing, starting and stopping, and naming moments for several minutes.

○ Begin to notice other people. Dance with someone for a moment and then move on to someone else. Energize the people with whom you connect with your focus and movement. Begin forming relationships. Continue observing, starting and stopping, and naming moments. For example, if you see a fellow student dancing near the chalkboard, you might say, "Mary dancing past chalkboard." Continue dancing, observing, starting and stopping, naming moments and forming relationships for several minutes.

○ When the music stops, ground and center, find natural alignment, connect with the breath and begin "The archer".

Bibliography

Books

Barton, Robert, and Dal Vera, Rocco, Voice Onstage and Off, 2nd edn. New York and Oxford: Routledge, 2011.

Berry, Cecily, *The Actor and the Text*. Montclair: Applause Theatre Books, 2000.

Boston, Jane, and Cook, Rena, eds, *Breath in Action: The Art of Breath in Vocal and Holistic Practice*. London: Jessica Kinsley Publishers, 2009.

Bunch, Meribeth, *The Dynamics of the Singing Voice*, 4th edn. New York: SpringerWein, 1997.

Carey, David, and Clark Carey, Rebecca, *Vocal Arts Workbook and DVD*. London: Methuen Drama, 2008.

———, *Verbal Arts Workbook*. London: Methuen Drama, 2010.

Cazden, Joanna, *How to Take Care of Your Voice: The Lifestyle Guide for Singers and Talkers*. Bangor: www.Booklocker.com, 2008.

Colaianni, Louis, *The Joy of Phonetics and Accents*. New York: Drama Book Publishers, 1994.

Davies, D. Garfield, *Care of the Professional Voice: A Guide to Voice Management for Singers, Actors and Professional Voice Users*. New York: Routledge, 2005.

DeVore, Kate, and Cookman, Starr, *The Voice Book*. Chicago: Chicago Review Press, 2009.

Gronbeck-Tedesco, John, *Acting Through Exercises*. Mountain View: Mayfield Publishing Company, 1992.

Kayes, Gillyanne, *Singing and the Actor*, 2nd edn. London: A & C Black, 2004.

Kopf, Ginny, *The Dialect Handbook*. Orlando: Voiceprint Publishing, 1997.

Lewis, Dennis, *The Tao of Natural Breathing*. San Francisco: Mountain Wind Publishing, 1997.

Linklater, Kristin, *Freeing the Natural Voice*. Hollywood: Drama Publishers, 2006.

McAvenue, Kelly, *The Actor and the Alexander Technique*. New York: Palgrave Macmillan, 2002.

Meier, Paul, *Accents and Dialects for the Stage and Screen*. Lawrence: Paul Meier Dialect Service, 2009.

Parkin, Ken, *Anthology of British Tongue-Twisters*. London: Samuel French, 1969.

Rodenburg, Patsy, *The Actor Speaks*. London: Methuen Drama, 1997.

———, *The Right to Speak*. New York: Routledge, 1992.

———, *Speaking Shakespeare*. New York: Palgrave Macmillan, 2002.

Roth, Gabrielle, *Maps to Ecstasy: A Healing Journey for the Untamed Spirit*. Novato: New World Library, 1998.

Speads, Carola, *Ways to Better Breathing*. Rochester: Healing Arts Press, 1992.

Articles

Cook, Rena, "A Week with Andrew Wade", *Shakespeare Around the Globe*. Voice and Speech Review, 2005.

———, "Resonance", *Dramatics Magazine*, Educational Theatre Association, Vol. 78, No. 9 (May 2007).

Espinosa, Micha, "A Call to Action: Embracing the Cultural Voice or Taming the Wild Tongue", *A World of Voice*. Voice and Speech Review, 2011.

Knight, Dudley, "The Articulate Actor", *Dramatics Magazine*, Educational Theatre Association, Vol. 79, No. 1 (September 2007).

Ocampo-Guzman, Antonio, "Alignment and the Actor", *Dramatics Magazine*, Educational Theatre Association, Vol. 78, No. 7 (March 2007).

Vivier, Judylee, "Inhale, Exhale", *Dramatics Magazine*, Educational Theatre Association, Vol. 78, No. 8 (April 2007).

Production photos

All photographs were taken by Sandra and John Bent for the University of Oklahoma School of Drama's University Theatre productions.

Index